# Stevie Wonder

*MUSICIAN*

Muhammad Ali

Maya Angelou

Josephine Baker

George Washington Carver

Ray Charles

Johnnie Cochran

Bill Cosby

Frederick Douglass

W.E.B. Du Bois

Jamie Foxx

Aretha Franklin

Marcus Garvey

Savion Glover

Alex Haley

Jimi Hendrix

Gregory Hines

Langston Hughes

Jesse Jackson

Magic Johnson

Scott Joplin

Coretta Scott King

Martin Luther King Jr.

Spike Lee

Malcolm X

Bob Marley

Thurgood Marshall

Barack Obama

Jesse Owens

Rosa Parks

Colin Powell

Condoleezza Rice

Chris Rock

Will Smith

Clarence Thomas

Sojourner Truth

Harriet Tubman

Nat Turner

Madam C.J. Walker

Booker T. Washington

Oprah Winfrey

Stevie Wonder

Tiger Woods

Black Americans of Achievement

*LEGACY EDITION*

# Stevie Wonder

*MUSICIAN*

Jeremy K. Brown

CHELSEA HOUSE
PUBLISHERS
An imprint of Infobase Publishing

**Stevie Wonder**

Copyright © 2010 by Infobase Publishing

Chelsea House
An imprint of Infobase Publishing
132 West 31st Street
New York, NY 10001

**Library of Congress Cataloging-in-Publication Data**

Brown, Jeremy K.
Stevie Wonder : musician / by Jeremy Brown.
    p.   cm. — (Black Americans of achievement. Legacy edition)
Includes bibliographical references and index.
ISBN 978-1-60413-685-2 (hardcover)
1. Wonder, Stevie—Juvenile literature.  2. African-American musicians—United States—Biography—Juvenile literature.  3. Soul musicians—United States—Biography—Juvenile literature.  4. Rhythm and blues musicians—United States—Biography—Juvenile literature. I. Title.  II. Series.
ML3930.W65B76 2010
782.421644092—dc22   [B]          2009050610

Chelsea House books are available at special discounts when purchased in bulk quantities for businesses, associations, institutions, or sales promotions. Please call our Special Sales Department in New York at (212) 967-8800 or (800) 322-8755.

You can find Chelsea House on the World Wide Web at http://www.chelseahouse.com.

Text design by Keith Trego
Cover design by Keith Trego
Composition by Keith Trego
Cover printed by Bang Printing, Brainerd, MN
Book printed and bound by Bang Printing, Brainerd, MN
Date printed: July 2010
Printed in the United States of America

10 9 8 7 6 5 4 3 2 1

This book is printed on acid-free paper.

All links and Web addresses were checked and verified to be correct at the time of publication. Because of the dynamic nature of the Web, some addresses and links may have changed since publication and may no longer be valid.

# Contents

# 1

# A Night of Wonder

**On January 20, 2009,** Barack Hussein Obama was sworn in as the forty-fourth president of the United States, capping off a jubilant period of celebration following his historic election. Obama's presidency signified a great many things to the people of America. Not only was the former U.S. senator from Illinois the first African American ever to be elected to the nation's highest office, but his campaign had been built around one word that resonated with voters everywhere: hope. In a time when the country's economy was ailing and unemployment rates skyrocketed, Obama's message of hope gave many Americans a sense that they had something to strive for, that things would get better.

To many in America, Obama represented a new kind of president. Far from being a stuffy politician in a pressed suit, Obama seemed youthful, hip, and in touch with young people. He played basketball, drank Pepsi, and carried around an iPod

**President Barack Obama presents Stevie Wonder with the Library of Congress Gershwin Award in the East Room of the White House in Washington, D.C., on February 25, 2009. The president is a longtime Stevie Wonder fan.**

plugged with artists ranging from Bob Dylan to Sheryl Crow. It was fitting then that, less than a month after his historic inauguration, President Obama hosted a special event in the East Room of the White House to present the second annual Gershwin Award for Lifetime Achievement to an artist who has been championing Obama's message of hope his entire life: Stevie Wonder.

"If I had one musical hero, it would have to be Stevie Wonder," Obama remarked to Jann Wenner in an interview for *Rolling Stone*. "When I was at that point where you start getting involved in music, Stevie had that run with *Music of My Mind, Talking Book, Fulfillingness' First Finale* and *Innervisions,* and then *Songs in the Key of Life*. Those are as brilliant a set of five albums as we've ever seen."

The award event was opulent and star-studded, with such famous names as Diana Krall, India.Arie, and Paul Simon on the guest list. Wonder himself rocked the East Room by playing his hit single "Sir Duke" from his legendary album *Songs in the Key of Life* and "Signed, Sealed, Delivered (I'm Yours)." Upon accepting the award, the singer was filled with his trademark humility and good humor. "I accept this in memory of my mother," he said. (His mother, Lula Mae Hardaway, had passed away only two years earlier.) "I know that Lula Mae is smiling right now, and Mr. President, I know if she were here, she'd say 'Let me get him a peach cobbler.'"

As lifelong fans of Stevie Wonder, Obama and his wife, Michelle, had chosen his song "You and I" as their wedding song. "I think it's fair to say that had I not been a Stevie Wonder fan, Michelle might not have dated me," President Obama said at the ceremony, as quoted in the *New York Times*. "We might not have married. The fact that we agreed on Stevie was part of the essence of our courtship."

Over the years, the first couple has turned to Wonder's music many times for comfort and encouragement. Speaking to Mark Silva of the *Chicago Tribune*'s Washington Bureau, Obama described the blind singer's music as being "the

## The Gershwin Prize for Popular Song

Named for renowned composers George and Ira Gershwin, the Library of Congress Gershwin Prize for Popular Song was created to recognize and honor popular music's influence on world culture. It is given to a composer whose body of work best typifies the high standards set by the Gershwins. Wonder is the second winner of the prize. The first was Paul Simon, who received the award in 2007.

soundtrack of my youth" and noted that it had helped him to find "peace and inspiration, especially in difficult times."

## A REMARKABLE JOURNEY

The notion of finding peace and inspiration in the face of adversity has marked the life and career of Stevie Wonder. Born blind and growing up with little money, Wonder overcame seemingly insurmountable odds to become one of the most prominent and respected performers and songwriters of the last five decades. His music transcends race and social boundaries, reaching into the homes of the rich and poor alike and stirring young and old minds with equal measure. He has influenced and impacted all genres of music—from pop, rap, and R&B to blues, funk, and jazz. Even country artists such as Carrie Underwood and opera singers such as the late Luciano Pavarotti have named Stevie Wonder as an influence. And he continues to inspire young musicians. Joe Jonas of the popular band The Jonas Brothers, singing Stevie Wonder's praises, said, "I still can't believe we [played] with him at the Grammys. He moves an audience."

In addition to being an accomplished singer and performer, Stevie Wonder has earned a reputation for being a champion of numerous causes, large and small. He has used his not-inconsiderable clout to draw attention to such issues as racism, segregation, war, famine, poverty, and apartheid in South Africa, among many others. His incredible musical output, positive message, and tireless activism have left even the most prestigious artists in awe. "He's so multitalented that it's hard to pinpoint exactly what it is that makes him one of the greatest ever," British songwriting sensation Elton John noted in *Rolling Stone*, adding:

> Stevie is an amazingly positive, peaceful man. When you ask him to do something, he is generous. He loves music. He loves to play. When he comes into a room, people adore him.

**From left, Kevin, Joe, and Nick Jonas of The Jonas Brothers perform with Stevie Wonder at the Fifty-first Annual Grammy Awards on February 8, 2009, in Los Angeles, California.**

And there aren't many artists like that. People admire you and they like your records, but they don't want to stand up and hug you. But this man is a good man. He tries to use his music to do good. His message, I think, is about love, and in the world we live in today, that message does shine through.

# 2

# Born into Darkness

**Although Stevie Wonder has been** blind since infancy, it is highly probable that he was not born that way. He was born Steveland Hardaway Judkins on May 13, 1950, in Saginaw, Michigan. (His name was later changed to Steveland Morris after his mother's remarriage.) Stevie was a premature baby and was placed in an incubator. This situation may have contributed to his blindness. "I have a dislocated nerve in one eye, and a cataract in the other," he explained. "It may have happened from being in the incubator too long and receiving too much oxygen. You see, I was born prematurely by one full month. But a girl who was born on the same day that I was was also put into the incubator, and she died. I personally think that I'm lucky to be alive."

There is also evidence to suggest that Stevie's premature birth may have resulted in the blood vessels in his eyes not being able to grow fully, a condition known as retinopathy of prematurity (ROP). Previously known as retrolental fibroplasia (RLF), ROP is an eye disease that occurs exclusively in babies born prematurely. While its exact cause is unknown, many believe that a disordered growth of the retinal blood vessels may lead to scarring and, in serious cases, retinal detachment. During the 1940s and 1950s, there was a rash of ROP cases, with close to 12,000 premature children suffering blindness as a result of the disease.

In some cases, ROP is mild and does not cause long-term issues. In Stevie's case, however, his blindness was permanent. Over the years, he has refused to let his inability to see limit him in any way. Though he cannot see the ordinary things that people with sight take for granted, he remains philosophical about his condition. "In my mind, I can see all of these things in my own way," he says, "in the manner that we [blind people] can see them."

Stevie's mother, Lula Mae Hardaway, was saddened by her son's blindness and spent several years attempting to find methods to treat it. For a time following the diagnosis, Lula sought treatment from various faith healers who prayed over Stevie's eyes, willing them to be whole again. But in time, she came to grips with her son's disability, as did Stevie. "When I

### DID YOU KNOW?

Stevie Wonder is not the only famous person affected by ROP. Tom Sullivan, an actor and author, was born in 1947 prematurely and also suffered retinal detachment due to an overabundance of oxygen in his incubator. Just like Stevie, Sullivan overcame his disability and later became famous for his recurring role as Frank Riley on *Highway to Heaven* and such motivational books as 2003's *Seeing Lessons: 14 Life Secrets I've Learned Along the Way*.

was young," he once said, "my mother taught me never to feel sorry for myself, because handicaps are really things to be used, another way to benefit yourself and others in the long run."

Despite giving such sage advice, Lula continued to struggle with her son's disability, until his own wisdom dispelled her heartache. "I know it used to worry my mother," he said years later, "and I know she prayed for me to have sight someday, and so finally I just told her that I was *happy* being blind, and I thought it was a gift from God, and I think she felt better after that."

This sense of happiness in the face of terrible circumstances proved to be a thread that would carry on well into the musician's adult years. "I'm glad I'm blind," Wonder remarked in an interview with Ben Fong-Torres for *Rolling Stone*. "Being blind, you don't judge books by their covers. You go through things that are relatively insignificant and you pick out the things that are more important."

## Lula Mae Hardaway

Lula Mae Hardaway was not just the mother of Steveland Morris, she was in many ways the woman who gave the world Stevie Wonder. Born in Alabama in 1930, Hardaway was a hard worker who passed along her tireless ethic to her children. When Stevie was born blind, Lula refused to allow him to become a shut-in and instead sought new outlets for the child, most notably music. From that point on, Lula became a guiding influence in Stevie's life, even cowriting some of his hits, such as "I Was Made to Love Her" and most famously "Signed, Sealed, Delivered (I'm Yours)." When he won the Grammy Award for Album of the Year, Wonder would not take to the stage to accept the award unless his mother was there as well. When she came out, he handed her his Grammy, telling those in attendance: "Her strength has led us to this place."

Wonder eventually purchased a house for his mother in California's San Fernando Valley, where she lived for the remainder of her life. Lula passed away on June 10, 2006, at the age of 76.

From left to right, Little Richard, Stevie Wonder's mother, Lula Mae Hardaway, Wonder, and Chuck Berry at the Grammy Awards in Hollywood, on March 2, 1974. Wonder has described his mother as being central to his development as a musician.

## CHILDHOOD CHALLENGES

The other piece of the difficult puzzle that made up Stevie's childhood was the presence of his father, Calvin Judkins. A hard-living abusive man with a hair-trigger temper and little interest in supporting his family, Judkins did not take too kindly to having to raise a blind child. Lee Garrett, a childhood friend of Stevie's who was also blind, recalled talking to Lula years later, as recounted by Craig Werner in the book *Higher Ground: Stevie Wonder, Aretha Franklin, Curtis Mayfield and the Rise and Fall of American Soul.* He talked to her about the term "blind brat," a derogatory expression used to describe a child who was unwanted or uncared for as a result of blindness. "When I was telling Lula that story," Garrett said, "she shrugged her shoulders, saying she knew the expression 'the blind brat' only too well herself. If it were up to Judkins, Steve would have ended up in a corner, like myself."

In time, and perhaps in defiance of Judkins and others who would put limits on her son, Lula came to accept her son's condition and refused to allow it to keep him from having a normal life. She would encourage him to go out and play with his brothers and sister, roaming the neighborhood in search of the normal adventures that every young boy seeks. "I always loved her for giving me that independence," he later said, as quoted by Werner. "She let me feel the freedom of riding a bicycle."

Stevie has recalled that his brothers were good to him and never let his handicap keep him from playing with them. In fact, as he once recalled, they even once attempted a rather

## IN HIS OWN WORDS...

**Stevie Wonder has never thought of his blindness as a handicap. In fact, he once said:**

I sometimes feel I am really blessed to be blind because I probably would not last a minute if I were able to see things. God knew what he was doing.

radical method to help their stricken brother regain his sight. "When I was just a little baby, I remember my brothers Milton and Calvin were messing around with a lot of stuff in the house, they had stuff all over everywhere jam and bubble gum and stuff," he said.

> They had a garbage can and some matches in the house, and they were saying, "God, you know what Stevie needs some more light. Wonder what we can do to get him some light? Maybe we can set this thing . . . like start a fire in here and he'll have some more light." So they went and started a fire and almost blew the house down.

Empowered by his mother's acceptance and emboldened by his brothers' freewheeling rambunctious sensibility, Stevie set about exploring his world, climbing up apple trees and racing his bike downhill, using another rider to handle the steering. As he grew braver, Stevie began to take greater and greater leaps of faith, sometimes quite literally. "You know those small sheds they used to have in the backs of houses?" he once recalled. "In the ghetto where I lived, we'd hop from them from one to the other."

Stevie's recklessness oftentimes resulted in severe repercussions, usually in the form of what he later would refer to as a "whumping" from his mother. Even in the face of such corporal punishment, however, his brashness represented a step forward in living with blindness. Without his eyes to guide him, Stevie began to rely on his other senses, most notably his hearing. For instance, during his "shed jumping" escapade, Stevie would call out and then listen. If a rooftop was close enough to jump to, it would sound one way. If it were too far away, it would sound completely different. In this way, it was almost as though he were using a form of sonar, using sound rather than sight to be his guide, similar to the way bats do in the wild.

As he grew, Stevie continued to hone his hearing, filtering out sounds so that he could, in essence, "see" with his ears. An example of this came when Stevie was a small boy. "I remember people dropping money on the table, and saying, 'What's that, Stevie?' That's a dime—buh-duh-duh-da: that's a quarter—buh-duh-duh-duh-dah; that's a nickel. I could almost always get it right except a penny and a nickel confused me."

Stevie's ears eventually became so highly trained that he could differentiate everything from birds to people's moods, all by the sounds they made and the tone of their voice. He could even tell various trees apart just by hearing how the wind rustled through their leaves. Yet, just as these victories represented a tremendous turning point for Stevie, a whole host of other challenges were about to present themselves.

## MOVING TO DETROIT

When he was three years old, Stevie and his family left Saginaw for Detroit, Michigan. Life in the busy urban center was challenging for Stevie. Far from the comfortable and familiar environs of Saginaw, Stevie felt alone and isolated. To make matters worse, his mother's relationship with Stevie's father had deteriorated to a point where Calvin Judkins was largely absent from their lives. While for Lula this was a blessing, as Judkins had been a nightmarish presence in her life, the separation still made for a difficult adjustment for the children. Stevie would occasionally visit his father, but the meetings were often unpleasant. In Werner's book, Stevie recalled the aftermath of one particularly horrid exchange. "He stayed away for a long time and left me alone," he said. "I got upset and I started to cry about that. But after a while I just said, hey forget it, and I went on to sleep. I was just afraid because the surroundings weren't familiar to me."

Detroit presented other challenges to Stevie and his family. In the 1950s, the country was still gripped by racism. Hostility toward those of African-American descent was open and widespread, and jobs for black workers were hard to come by. Lulu worked tirelessly at several jobs in order to provide for her family, but money was still in short supply. In an interview with *Newsweek*, later quoted by Werner, Stevie recalled the family's desperate economic situation. "I would love to do a TV special that would tell many things people don't know about me," he said, "like how when I was younger my mother, my brothers and I had to go on the dry dock where there was coal and steal some to keep warm. To a poor person that is not stealing, that is not crime, it's a necessity."

Years later, Lula would claim the coal-stealing story was untrue, a point to which Stevie offered this explanation:

> My mother was unhappy with the reference to the fact that I stole coal when I was young. I'm not ashamed to talk about it, but my mother felt very bad. I tried to explain to her that I told the story only because it's sad that in a country that is as wealthy as the United States stealing for survival is a necessity as well as a *crime*.

## AN OUTSIDER EVEN IN SCHOOL

In addition to confronting poverty, Stevie also encountered hostility in the one place one would have thought he could have found acceptance—at school with fellow blind students. Even there, among similarly afflicted children, Stevie was made to feel like an outsider. The blind children at school had developed a hierarchy of sorts, in which those children who were partially sighted were superior to those who were totally blind, as Stevie was. These kids were referred to, in whispers and rebukes in the hallways, as "the blind kids" and were often ostracized from social circles. Even the teachers often made Stevie feel as though the odds were against him. "They made me feel like because I was black, I could never be or would never be successful," he later observed.

"I remember a teacher telling me that I should go on and make sure I studied very hard, because the only thing that I could probably do was tune pianos—no, I'm serious—or make baskets or potholders or rugs," he said in Werner's book.

> And this lady was being sincere. She didn't mean no harm by what she was saying. Being black and blind, that was all that was supposed to happen. They must have had visions of me being a hawker, peddling with shoelace and pencils or haunting some street corner with a Seeing-Eye dog begging for money or at the best sitting in some busy place playing the harmonica and holding a hat for alms.

Perhaps in an effort to prove all of those naysayers wrong or perhaps imbued with his mother's indomitable spirit, Stevie threw himself into his learning, mastering the art of reading Braille in school. Braille is a system of raised dots on a page, with six dots positioned in a rectangle representing a character. By using touch, a blind person can distinguish letters, numbers, and words and read sentences on a page. For his mastery of the language, Stevie was given a Braille Bible. Learning to read opened new worlds for Stevie and encouraged him to further enhance his sense of touch, adding it to the arsenal of senses he employed to navigate his world. "The sense of touch. I dig it," he later noted. "It's a way of bringing the world closer to me. It helps me give off good vibes."

Day by day, Stevie was adapting to his surroundings and facing every challenge that was presented to him. And soon he would see that, while the move to Detroit may have brought with it poverty, racism, and other hardships, it was about to open doors that might have otherwise remained forever closed.

# 3

# Music Lights the Way

**From an early age,** music had been an important part of Stevie Wonder's life. His mother, though not a professional, sang gospel music at the local church and encouraged her son's musical growth. When Stevie was two years old, his mother gave him a pair of spoons, which he quickly fashioned into drumsticks, beating rhythmically on everything in the house. "I was always beating things," he said later, as quoted in Werner's book, "like beating tables with a spoon, or beating on those little cardboard drums they used to give kids. I'd beat 'em to death."

Drums were of great interest to Stevie and represented one of his first ventures into music. At a neighborhood Christmas party one year, Stevie was given a drum set of his own. "I started playing the drums on the wrong side," he recalled. "So they came over to me and said, 'Hey, you don't do it like this, try it over on the other side' and I'd say, 'Oh no, I wanna hear the side with the snares!'"

As time went on, more and more instruments found their way into Stevie's home. After some neighbors who were moving out of the area gave their piano to the family, it was not long before Stevie was experimenting on the keys and learning to play various tunes.

But of all his musical explorations, perhaps the thing that ignited his musical career came when Stevie discovered the harmonica. His first exposure to the instrument came in the form of a tiny four-hole harmonica that dangled from a family friend's key chain. The item was little more than a novelty, but Stevie managed to get a fantastic range of sound out of it, so much so that he was soon presented with the real thing. From there, he never looked back. In order to develop as a harmonica player, he began listening to blues records by such artists as Jimmy Reed, Bobby "Blue" Bland, and Little Walter and imitating what he heard. "I started playing the blues," he said. "I took a little bit of everybody's style and made it my

## Musical Therapy

Music has long been an outlet for parents, teachers, and health-care providers looking to reach and comfort disabled, injured, or sick patients. According to the American Music Therapy Association, the practice of using music for therapeutic purposes began after the First World War, when musicians would visit the bedsides of wounded soldiers. Based on the positive responses seen in the patients, doctors began to hire musicians to work in hospitals on a regular basis. In 1944, during the Second World War, Michigan State University founded the first-ever music therapy degree program. Since then, music therapy has grown rapidly and has been used in a variety of ways. For example, Bedside Harp, a Pennsylvania-based organization, sends harpists to perform in hospitals, while the British organization Music for Autism uses music to improve the quality of life for children and parents dealing with autism. In 1998, the National Association for Music Therapy and the American Association for Music Therapy unified to form the American Music Therapy Association, which currently represents more than 5,000 music therapists.

own. I guess I practiced, but I never considered it practice because I loved it too much. It was like searching in a new place you've never been before. I kept finding new things, new chords, new tunes."

## ABSORBING MUSIC

Before long, music was the driving force in young Stevie's life, dominating nearly every one of his waking hours. If he was not playing it, he was listening to it. "I spent a lot of time listening to the radio," he said, "and I was able to relate to the different instruments and know what they were. I began to know them by name."

Rather than be content with only one style of music, Stevie listened to a wide range. "I listened to jazz stations, classical stations, even Polish stations," he said in an interview with Barney Hoskyns for *Uncut.* "I was just curious. I didn't limit myself. It could be Motown or it could be Neil Sedaka. It could be Charlie Parker or John Coltrane."

Stevie's love of music quickly blossomed into a love of performance. Many afternoons would find him out on his front porch, playing bongos or harmonica. Other people from the neighborhood would occasionally join these impromptu jam sessions, but Stevie's voice and musicality would always rise above all the others. "We used to get pretty big crowds on those porches," he said.

I remember this one time this lady who was a member of our church … the Whitestone Baptist Church, and she came along and she said, "Oh Stevie, I'm ashamed of you for playing that worldly music out here. I'm so ashamed of you." Ha, I really blew it, boy. I'd been a junior deacon in the church and I used to sing solo at the services. But she went and she told them what I was doing and they told me to leave. And that's how I became a sinner.

*(continues on page 20)*

## Blind Musicians

Although Stevie Wonder and Ray Charles are two of the most popular blind musicians of the modern era, many people without sight have turned to music as a suitable means of expression throughout history. In Ukraine, for example, there is a strong tradition of blind musical performance known as *kobzarstvo*. The performers, known as *kobzars*, generally became musicians because their disability did not allow them to work in any other job. Here are five musicians who rose above their blindness to make an impact:

### OSTAP VERESAI

Having lost his eyesight at age four, Veresai studied under various kobzars to become one of the most famous minstrels in Ukraine. During the mid-1800s, Veresai was the region's most popular kobzar, performing not only in Ukraine but also beyond its borders. His style of playing and versatility gave rise to a style of music known as *dumka*, which applies folk patterns to classical music forms. This style later influenced such composers as Antonin Dvorak and Pyotr Tchaikovsky.

The Blind Boys of Alabama, *(left to right)* Trey Pierce, Billy Bowers, Clarence Fountain, Jimmy Carter, and Joey Williams, perform at Fort Mason Great Meadow in San Francisco, California, on August 20, 2006. Although their lineup has changed through the decades, the group has been an inspiration for blind musicians everywhere, including Stevie Wonder.

### THE BLIND BOYS OF ALABAMA

Founded in 1939 by a group of musicians at the Alabama School for the Negro Blind, the Blind Boys of Alabama may be the longest-running group of blind performers still active today. Although only one founding member remains, vocalist Clarence Fountain, the band still tours and performs regularly. In addition to having shared the stage with such notable musicians as Peter Gabriel, Prince, and John Fogerty, their songs have been heard on TV programs such as *The Wire* and *Lost*.

### BLIND WILLIE JOHNSON

Though much of his life is shrouded in mystery, the impact that this legendary blues singer had on music is clear. Willie Johnson is today regarded as one of the finest, if not *the* finest, guitarists and songwriters of his, or any, time. His unmistakable style of guitar playing, sliding a metal or glass object against the strings to produce a series of unique tones, has become synonymous with the blues sound of the early twentieth century. Countless musical artists, including Led Zeppelin, Bob Dylan, and the White Stripes, have covered Johnson's songs. In 1977, Johnson's recording of "Dark Was the Night, Cold Was the Ground," was sent into space on the *Voyager 1* probe as one example of Earth's rich and diverse musical culture.

### RONNIE MILSAP

Country music's first blind star, Ronnie Milsap was also an artist who, much like Stevie Wonder, has been able to cross genres and reach fans outside of the country realm. With 40 number-one hits to his name, he is one of the most successful country singers in history. His songs "Smoky Mountain Rain," "It Was Almost Like a Song," and "She Keeps the Home Fires Burning" made him a household name throughout the 1970s and 1980s. Today he remains one of the biggest touring acts in the country.

### SCOTT MACINTYRE

The 25-year-old singer from California became the first visually impaired finalist in the history of *American Idol*. Though not fully blind (he retains 2 percent vision in his eyes), MacIntyre set a great example for those with visual disabilities. He recorded his first album when he was 11 and has since released a total of six albums, mostly on independent labels. On the *American Idol* singing competition, MacIntyre made it into the top eight finalists before being eliminated on April 8, 2009. Nevertheless, he joined his cast mates that summer on the American Idols LIVE! tour.

*(continued from page 17)*

Stevie's excommunication from the church was both a blow and a blessing to the young man. He had enjoyed performing in the choir, where his mother also sang, and had fostered a strong relationship with God, particularly in the wake of his blindness, poverty, and parental issues. Despite his parish's decision, he chose to remain hopeful, believing that his talent came from a higher place, and as such, had a higher calling. "I felt that if God didn't want me to sing it, he wouldn't have given me the talent to do it," he told Hoskyns. "I felt that if he didn't want me to know the difference between right and wrong, he wouldn't have given me a mother and people that loved me and nurtured me."

## DISCOVERY

Unable to sing in church, Stevie's public concerts were limited to the front porch. It was around this time that he began singing regularly with a boy his age named John Glover. "John and I had formed a group called 'Steve and John,'" he recalled in an interview with *Rock Around the World*:

> I would play bongos and John played guitar. I'd sing and John would play and do some of the harmonies with me. We did a lot of the songs of the fifties and sixties. We did "Once Upon A Time" and "Why Do Fools Fall In Love?" . . . I used to love to do the imitations of Jackie Wilson, and it was crazy because when I became aware of how Jackie Wilson performed, heard he was a very exciting performer—you know—I used to do all kinds of flips and stuff. I was about nine or ten years old then.

The pairing with Glover would prove to be more fortuitous for Stevie than he could have imagined. Glover's cousin was Ronnie White, a founding member of the Miracles, a rhythm and blues group that had been enjoying success at the time with such hit singles as "Shop Around" and "You Really Got a Hold on Me."

Believing Stevie had talent enough to make it as a professional musician, Glover contacted White and asked that he come down to hear him sing. Because White was not convinced that an 11-year-old child was really worth his time, he postponed the visit several times. Finally, unable to put it off any longer, White came down to hear one of the boys' front-porch concerts. Almost immediately, he recognized the immenseness of Stevie's musical ability and arranged for a meeting at the headquarters of Tamla Records, the Miracles' Detroit-based record label.

Although still a child, Steveland Morris was about to have his life changed forever.

# 4

# Motown Bound

**Berry Gordy had founded** Tamla Records in 1959 after spending years as a songwriter for local Detroit musicians such as Jackie Wilson, whose hit "Lonely Teardrops" was written by Gordy.

Realizing that the real way to make money in the music business was to be on the producing and publishing side, Gordy quickly formed Tamla (the name was inspired by the Debbie Reynolds song "Tammy"), using an $800 loan from his family. The label operated out of a former photographer's studio in a building that quickly became known as "Hitsville, U.S.A." In 1960, Gordy would change the label's name from Tamla to Motown. The name, a fusion of "Motor" and "Town," was a reference to Detroit's then-booming automobile manufacturing business.

The first act Gordy signed to the new label was the Miracles. Formerly known as the Matadors, the group, led by the charismatic singer Smokey Robinson, quickly became a success and

**Smokey Robinson (left) expresses his delight as he is joined by Berry Gordy at the Greek Theater in Los Angeles, California, on June 15, 1981. As president and founder of Motown Records, Gordy built a portfolio of successful recording artists, including Robinson and a very young Stevie Wonder.**

paved the way for countless other acts, helping to create what is now known as the "Motown Sound."

Having been impressed with young Stevie's talent, Ronnie White brought him to Hitsville in 1961 to introduce him to Gordy. In his 1994 autobiography, *To Be Loved*, Gordy wrote of first seeing the young musician. "He was singing, playing the bongos and blowing on a harmonica," Gordy recalled. "His voice didn't knock me out, but his harmonica playing did. Something about him was infectious."

Stevie's talent shone that day, and it was plain to everyone present that there was something special about this child. "I

## Berry Gordy and Motown

Michael Jackson, Diana Ross, Marvin Gaye, and Stevie Wonder—these artists, among many, many others, have one thing in common: They might never have been heard from had it not been for Berry Gordy. A high school dropout, Gordy first sought his fortune as a professional boxer before being drafted into the army during the Korean War. After the war ended in 1953, Gordy worked for a time as the owner of a record store but started writing songs after meeting Jackie Wilson at a local nightclub. Gordy composed several songs for Wilson, most famously "Lonely Teardrops," before parlaying his songwriting success into a role as a record producer. Armed with $800 and a newly discovered singing group, The Matadors (later called the Miracles), Gordy formed Tamla records, which soon became Motown.

Over the years, Gordy proved himself to have a keen eye for talent, discovering and signing many of music's most famous and enduring names. He also helped to streamline the Motown sound, drawing on gospel influences and layering in horn and string arrangements. Another key element to Motown's success was the label's image, presenting clean-cut singers in pressed suits and dresses who sang and danced in perfectly choreographed routines.

After moving the headquarters of Motown from Detroit to Los Angeles in the late 1960s, Gordy transitioned from record producer to movie producer, overseeing such hits as *Lady Sings the Blues* (1972), *Mahogany* (1975), and *The Last Dragon* (1985). In addition, he continued to discover new musical talents, including The Jackson 5, New Edition, and Boyz II Men.

Although now retired, Gordy continues to remain a presence in the music world, most recently speaking at the memorial for Michael Jackson on July 7, 2009. His label celebrated its fiftieth anniversary in 2009, with reissues of many of its signature albums and a boxed set of number-one singles. Today, the only artist on the Motown label who was signed during its heyday is Stevie Wonder.

think his mother was with him, and a couple of brothers," said Mary Wilson of the Supremes. "He's just a typical ten-year-old, comes running in, so Berry says, 'Can you play this instrument?' So he played the piano. He played the organ. He played the drums, the congas. He played everything there. And Berry said, 'You are signed.'"

## MINGLING AT MOTOWN

Stevie was signed shortly after his meeting with Gordy under the name Little Stevie Wonder. There has long been debate as to where Stevie's stage name came from. Some sources credit producer Mickey Stevenson, while others say it was Gordy himself who came up with the name. In his autobiography, Gordy writes, "I don't really remember it, but [my sister] Esther told me that one day in the studio, watching Stevie perform, I said, 'Boy! That kid's a wonder,' and the name stuck."

Now known by his stage name, Stevie finally felt as though he was in a place where he truly belonged. Hitsville was like a candy factory to a boy as enamored with music as Stevie was. Every day, there were new instruments to play, new sounds to create, and new ways to indulge in his favorite pastime. "It was like a music store with all kinds of toys," he recalled.

Around the Hitsville building, the energetic musical prodigy became something of a company mascot. The more seasoned musicians took Stevie under their wings and looked after him. Before long, Stevie was palling around the who's who of the burgeoning Motown scene. Talking with Craig Werner in *Goldmine*, Wonder remembered those glory days. "Martha Reeves used to show me all the new dances to do," he recalled.

> I was very fortunate to meet a family like the Gordy family, like Motown. Everyone over 11 was a parent. [Producer] Clarence Paul loved me like his own son. He was like a father, like a brother and friend. Esther Edwards, Berry Gordy's sister . . . all the musicians and artists watched over

An early 1960s portrait of Stevie Wonder in a recording studio. Although recognized as a musical prodigy, Wonder spent several years at Motown trying out various musical styles before he came into his own as a musician.

me. Wanda [Young] of the Marvelettes would always tell me when she thought I was eating too much candy. I wish kids today could have the same kind of caring expressed and shown to them.

Oftentimes after a session, Stevie would find himself waiting for a ride home. During those times, he would head over to the Reeves' house, where he quickly charmed the family with his youthful exuberance. "He knew and loved my family just like he's a member, because we took him in," Martha Reeves recalled. "It's not like he was a little blind kid. Stevie was active! Stevie would beat everybody up; he was taller than most of them. They'd tear my mama's house up."

In Werner's book, Reeves also remembers Stevie's penchant for creating songs on the Hammond organ and recording them on the family tape recorder: "He'd play those silly chords and talk over them, make up dumb stories."

Though a gifted musician, Stevie still *was* a child, and as such was prone to the occasional act of mischief. On one occasion, Stevie's troublemaking led to an incident that, had it been discovered, would have cost him his career:

> Me and my friend, after a couple of days we kept going down [to Hitsville], and we went into the basement and stole some tapes. This is something Motown probably never knew I did, but it's cool now. I stole—it must have been a two-track of "Shop Around" by the Miracles. I kept it—I think we tore it up or something. But they were asking me, "Steve, have you seen it? Somebody stole a tape. Where's the tape?" And I just never did say anything about it. 'Cause I thought I'd lose my contract.

One of his gifts, in addition to music, was mimicry. "He could do all kinds of accents and voices," Gordy recalled. "Including mine." In fact, imitating Gordy was a particular pastime of Stevie's, and on more than one occasion, the young musician tried to use it to his advantage. Gordy recalled:

> He'd call my secretary and say, "Send Stevie Wonder a check for a half million dollars right away. He needs the money right away." So my secretary says, "Wait a minute, boss. Just like that?" "Yes, just like that, and do it right away." She says, "Have you lost your mind?" He says, "No, Stevie's my friend, Stevie's a fine young man, just give him a check. He'll be in there shortly." I don't think he got any checks, but who knows?

In spite of all the fun he was having at Hitsville, Stevie had been signed to make music. In 1962, he released his first album, *The Jazz Soul of Little Stevie Wonder*. The album has no vocal tracks and is primarily a showcase of Stevie's prodigious musical talent. He plays harmonica, drums, and keyboards on the record and even helped write a few of the songs. Although the album did not fare well on the charts, many people acknowledged it was an impressive debut for so young an artist.

Stevie's next album for Tamla, *Tribute to Uncle Ray*, was designed as an homage to Ray Charles, a man to whom Stevie felt a strong kinship. He admitted in an interview with Hoskyns, "I didn't know for the longest time that Ray Charles was blind." Wonder told Hoskyns:

> It was only when I was 11 and I did the *Tribute to Uncle Ray* album and they put this Braille on there that I found out. When I was around eight or nine, my mother took me to see him at the Michigan State Fairgrounds, and then later when I met him, it was a wonderful moment. It was on a Sunday, and I think it was at the Ford Auditorium, must have been like '62.... He came out of his dressing room, and some people were leading him over to me. He was kinda laughing and jumping up and down a little bit. And I presented him with the album, and he said, "Keep on doing what you're

doing, young man." And his drummer gave me a pair of drumsticks. I was so happy.

Again the record showcased Stevie's considerable musical ability, but it failed to generate any real hits and did not provide the breakout success that Gordy had been hoping for. The label was still trying to find a sound for Stevie, something that would click with audiences.

## FIRST TOUR

In order to introduce Stevie to the world, Gordy put him on the Motown Revue tour, the package concert tours of Motown artists in the 1960s. For the Motown performers, this tour was a grueling series of one-night stands across the country. Gordy wanted to bring the Motown sound to America and that meant getting as much exposure as possible. One famous stint had the Revue performing a weeklong stand at the Apollo Theater in Harlem in New York City, consisting of six shows a day starting at noon and ending at one the following morning.

Throughout this cross-country grind, Stevie provided some much needed relief from the tension of the road. His good humor and excitement at living the life of a traveling musician was infectious. Writing in his autobiography, *Temptations*, Otis Williams of the Temptations remembered:

> The one guy everybody loved was Stevie Wonder. Stevie loved to make people laugh and had an impish charm. Usually he sat at the back of the bus with the musicians and played his harmonica for hours. Everyone understood he was wood-shedding [a musician's term meaning to practice your skills], but only to a point. When it got to be about two or three in the morning, someone would yell, "Stevie, man, put that damn harmonica down and go to sleep." If that didn't work, we tried, "Stevie, we're going to beat [you

up] if you don't take that harmonica . . ." and he'd laugh, because he knew we'd never do that. Not that the thought didn't cross our minds now and then.

As joyful as life on the road was for Stevie, reality was hard to escape. As a minor, Stevie was still legally obligated to attend school. Just as his career was getting off the ground, the Detroit Board of Education informed Stevie that he would be unable to continue his music career. The news broke the young singer's heart. "I cried and cried and prayed for a long time," he told Werner.

Eventually, through the help of Lula and the Michigan School for the Blind, a solution was reached. Stevie would travel with a tutor, Ted Hull, who would be in charge of Stevie's education and also look after the young man while he was on the road, making sure he avoided trouble and providing him with an allowance of $2.50 a week.

For Hull, a teacher who himself was visually impaired, to go from the Michigan School for the Blind to traveling America with the Motown Revue was a bit of a culture shock. Hull told Werner:

> Stevie held out extremely well, and I always recognized that he was holding down two full-time jobs, one as a student, one as an entertainer. I don't think he realized it. We wouldn't start school until about ten o'clock in the morning, but I would get up at six A.M. usually to prepare for school—to get a head start on the kid. Then we would have school for three and a half or four hours, and then it would be the entertainment business until maybe twelve or one o'clock in the evening. So I was absolutely exhausted.

Life on the highways of America was fun and exciting for Stevie, but also overwhelming. Looking back, he has expressed gratitude for having people like Hull around him. "There was anxiety sometimes," he told Hoskyns.

You hear people playing and having fun and being silly, and you want to be a part of that. But thank God I had people like Ted Hull, who was a great teacher and mentor, and Ardena Johnston, who was my chaperone and was a great mother on the road for a long time. Clarence Paul, who was doing his thing and was a little wild, made sure that I stayed in line. Really everyone was cool. Obviously they allowed me to discover certain things at the right age. I would not change anything about my life at that time. Every single one of those people played a significant part in wherever I am now.

During this time with the Motown Revue, Stevie began developing his onstage persona, growing more comfortable with playing in front of a live audience. "The first time I began to feel I was exciting to people, I threw my glasses out into the audience," he remembered. "I used to have a bow tie on. I threw that out. It was so exciting that I wanted to get them to do it again, so the next night, I tried it again, and it was still exciting."

His high-energy antics onstage soon gave rise to character traits that would come to be instantly identified with Stevie Wonder, such as swaying from side to side in time with the music and rocking back and forth. These movements, called "blindisms," are a blind person's way of compensating for a lack of sight. "When you're blind you build up a lot of excess energy that other people get rid of through their eyes," he once remarked. "You got to work it off some way, you know, and it's just an unconscious thing. Like, a lot of blind people are always rubbing their eyes. Each person develops his own blindism."

### "FINGERTIPS—PART 2"

In 1963, Stevie was performing before a raucous crowd in Chicago, playing the single "Fingertips" from the *Jazz Soul* album. The song is mostly a call-and-answer number, with Stevie shouting out "yeah, yeah, yeah," then blowing the harmonica as the crowd answers back and the band kicks in to a fast-paced rhythm and blues number. A staple of Stevie's set, "Fingertips" had never failed to whip audiences into a frenzy. "When Stevie got to 'Fingertips,' the closing tune, people jumped up and down, clapped their hands, and stomped their feet," reported Brian Holland, a Motown singer and songwriter. "They just went wild. The atmosphere was pure electricity, that's how great Stevie was. . . . At the end, it seemed, they were more exhausted by all the hand-clapping stuff they did than Stevie was."

On this particular night in the Windy City, the energy of the crowd was palpable, as was Stevie's onstage liveliness. In fact, the song, as it was released, almost happened by accident. The band had finished playing "Fingertips" and left the stage. But Stevie, as he was being escorted off, raced back out and began to play again. His band, assuming this was part of the act, simply joined in. The only problem was, Stevie's bassist had already left. As a result, Larry Moses, the bassist for another Motown artist, Mary Wells, had to jump in. As the band played, Moses frantically yelled out, "What key? What key?" trying to get in tune with his fellow musicians. The madcap scene onstage added to the record's off-the-cuff feel, and Gordy opted to leave it in. "We're not sure why the record was such a big hit," Gordy recalled in his autobiography, "but leaving that mistake in didn't hurt. There are certain kinds of mistakes I love."

The song, now called "Fingertips—Part 2," quickly became a smash single, rocketing to number one on the charts and becoming Tamla's biggest-selling single. The album on which "Fingertips—Part 2" was included, *Recorded Live: The 12 Year Old Genius,* was also a hit, bringing Stevie to the forefront of the music scene almost overnight. To this day, Stevie is the youngest artist ever to have an album reach number one on the charts.

The single put Stevie Wonder on the map. Though not yet a teenager, Stevie had gone from being a blind, disadvantaged child from the inner city to a bona fide recording star.

# 5

# Teenage Superstar

**Throughout his childhood, Stevie had** to deal with his blindness. Now he faced a new hurdle: fame. While being a well-known singer had its advantages, it was also completely new to Stevie. Whereas before he had felt isolated and alone, it now seemed that everyone in the world wanted to be his friend. Elaine Jesmer, one of Stevie's chaperones, remembered a time in Los Angeles that showed just how famous Stevie Wonder had become. "We pulled up at 103rd Street and we just let him out," Jesmer recalled.

> He just stood there and people started coming over. Stevie was like a magnet. People would go up to him and they would touch him and he would touch them back. They didn't talk a lot, it was more like "Oh my God, this is really Stevie Wonder." The feeling from them to him and the other way round was just like magic. I remember one little boy who was walking around the street corner and when he

saw Stevie he stopped dead. He just looked at Stevie and his mouth fell open and his eyes got really big and then he looked at me and he wanted to say something but he couldn't. And I just nodded my head. That very second the boy turned around and took off. But then, about five minutes later, he came back and he must have brought about twenty-five other kids with him—all between twelve and fourteen years old. And they were all over Stevie. It was an incredible scene. Everybody wanted to touch Stevie or take his hand.

Unfortunately for Stevie, fame also had its downside. The repercussions of having a famous member of the family were hard on Stevie's relatives, who were still living in the same Detroit neighborhood. Longtime friend Lee Garrett recalled to Werner:

[S]ome people in the neighborhood got really nasty. They envied Stevie and his family so much that they would try anything to make them unhappy. Especially the young ones, [his siblings] Larry, Timothy, and Renee, who were then twelve, ten, and four years old, had to suffer from neighbors' hate. . . . They either found themselves surrounded by children who wanted to get to Stevie through them, or they would have vicious neighbors or even their kids say terrible things to them. And believe me, it did get to [Stevie]. He wished so much that he could do something about it. But he knew that for the time being his hands were tied and the only thing he could do was to set his aims high, so that one day he would really have enough money to get his family out of all this hassle and away from those people who hurt their feelings.

During this period, as he traveled the country, Stevie was also becoming more aware of issues surrounding race. In the 1960s,

# Segregation

When Stevie Wonder traveled through the South during the early part of the 1960s, he witnessed firsthand some of the racial difficulties that plagued the region for nearly a century. Since the end of the Civil War in 1865, much of the United States still had "Jim Crow" laws in effect. These laws allowed for the separation of black and white people, forcing African Americans to use different restrooms, ride in the backs of public buses, and even drink from separate water fountains. Outrage over these laws led to the civil-rights movement, beginning in the mid-1950s. Spearheaded by such notable figures as Martin Luther King Jr., Medgar Evers, and Rosa Parks, the movement helped black Americans gain legal equality in American society. King's famous "I Have a Dream" speech—a plea for equality given on the steps of the Lincoln Memo-

On August 28, 1963, Dr. Martin Luther King Jr. acknowledges the crowd at the Lincoln Memorial during the March on Washington.

rial in Washington, D.C., on August 28, 1963—is considered to be one of the defining moments of the civil-rights era. The efforts of King and other activists led to the abolition of Jim Crow laws with the Civil Rights Act of 1964 and the Voting Rights Act of 1965. Though racist attitudes were still prevalent in some regions of the United States, the legal rights of African Americans as U.S. citizens could no longer be infringed upon.

segregation was still rampant in the South, and Stevie and the other African-American musicians in the Motown Revue were often subjected to unfair and cruel treatment at the hands of prejudiced people. "Down in Alabama, somebody shot a gun at the bus and just missed the gas tank," Stevie recalled.

> I remember once in Macon, GA, in 1963 or 1964, . . . there was a Confederate flag hanging over the stage. We had this cat, Gene Shelby, and he told this one guy, "Our big star Marvin Gaye ain't gonna like that flag." This guy says, "Hey boy, see the way that flag's blowin' in the breeze? If you don't get your tail out of here, your tail's gonna be up a tree blowin' just like that flag."

Experiences like this helped to open Stevie's mind to the division between races and would influence his music greatly. He began to write songs that spoke about how people could work together to heal their differences.

### LOOKING FOR ANOTHER HIT

Although "Fingertips—Part 2" made Stevie a sensation, finding a follow-up hit proved difficult. Gordy was still trying to find a way to package the young man to the record-buying public. A brief foray into surf music, captured on both the 1964 album *Stevie at the Beach* and in appearances in the films *Bikini Beach* and *Muscle Beach Party*, also failed to connect. "We hadn't taken advantage of it," Gordy recalled, talking about capitalizing on the success of "Fingertips—Part 2." "That was a no-no for our company. As far as I was concerned, that was a sin. As hard as it is to establish an act, once you do, once you open that door, you just have to march right through. With Stevie we hadn't and now it seemed we couldn't."

Approaching his fifteenth birthday, Stevie was already being seen by some critics as a one-off novelty. Songwriter Sylvia Moy remembered this period in an interview with Werner:

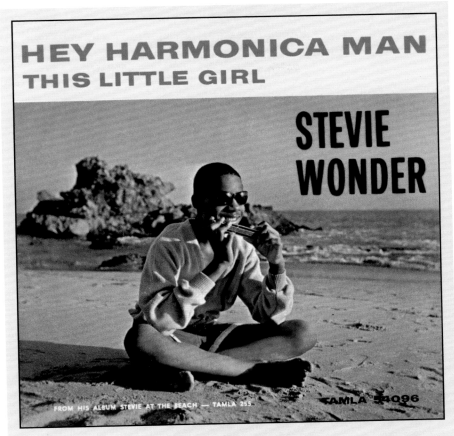

Shown here, the record sleeve for "Hey Harmonica Man," a single that sought to match Stevie Wonder with the surf music craze of the 1960s. The single peaked at number 29 on the charts in the summer of 1964.

"They would go through the list of artists and give assignments to the various producers. In 1965, no one wanted Stevie." The downtime did not affect Stevie, however. "I was too busy working on songs and listening to things and hearing ideas," he said.

The Motown label officials stuck by Stevie and worked with him until they could find for him the songs that would best demonstrate his talent and ability. They found those songs in the 1965 album *Up-Tight (Everything's Alright)*. Regarded as Stevie's breakthrough, the album featured "Uptight (Everything's Alright)," which proved to be the singer's biggest hit since "Fingertips—Part 2" almost three years earlier. Moy remembered how the single came about:

> I had a bag of songs at the time, but I told Stevie, "I want you to play everything, all of the little ditties you have, play them for me." He went through everything. He said, "That's all I have," and I thought I was going to have to start working from my bag. I asked him, "Are you sure you don't have anything else?" He said, "No, not really, although I have got this one thing." He started singing and playing, "Everything is alright, uptight," and that was as much as he had. I said, "That's it. Let's work with that."

The album was also notable for including Stevie's cover of Bob Dylan's "Blowin' in the Wind." A sensitive, introspective song about peace in times of war, the folk song did not fit in with the established Motown sound, and many questioned its inclusion on the album. But the song was important to Stevie, as he felt it represented his growth as an artist and his desire to have his music speak about larger issues in the world apart from girls and love. As it turned out, his instincts were correct,

## DID YOU KNOW?

"Blowin' in the Wind," which Stevie Wonder performed on his *Up-Tight (Everything's Alright)* album, is a song that has been covered by numerous artists, including Peter, Paul & Mary, Elvis Presley, John Fogerty, and Dolly Parton (who recorded it with bluegrass singers Nickel Creek in 2005). The song's first line, "How many roads must a man walk down?" is also humorously used as the "Ultimate Question" to life in the science-fiction novel *The Hitchhiker's Guide to the Galaxy* by Douglas Adams.

and the song became a top-10 hit. "I never felt that I strictly embodied the Motown sound," he said, regarding the controversial song choice. "I mean there weren't too many people around there doing white-folk stuff like 'Blowin' in the Wind,' or 'Mr. Tambourine Man' like I was."

If anyone doubted Stevie's inclusion of the Dylan song on his album, those doubts were erased when he performed the song live. Writer Rochelle Larkin remembered being at a concert that was not going well for the Motown performers:

> Outdoors in an enormous baseball field, horrible acoustics, cold and rainy. By the end of the first half, everyone, including the promoters, had wished they'd stayed home. Toward the end of the second half, Stevie Wonder came out and sang "Blowin' in the Wind" as if that song had never been sung before. Suddenly he wasn't "Little" Stevie Wonder anymore. He came out of the child-entertainer, novelty category and brought the crowd to its feet. He had reached for something and had caught it, and there was no longer a boy wonder, but a man.

# 6

# Years of Change

**As the sixties went on,** Stevie Wonder became a hit-making machine for the Motown label. Singles such as "I Was Made to Love Her," "Shoo-Be-Doo-Be-Doo-Da-Day," and "My Cherie Amour" not only were successful, but also became lasting pieces of his musical repertoire. One of these hit songs, "Signed, Sealed, Delivered (I'm Yours)," was partially credited to his mother, Lula, as she came up with the song's title after hearing her son play the riff.

As he was racking up hits, Wonder was also changing musically. He was no longer the "12 Year Old Genius," but a young man with things to say and a great pool of influences outside the "Motown Sound" to draw upon. Helping matters was the fact that the 1960s was a very rich time for pop music, with artists like The Beatles, The Rolling Stones, and Jimi Hendrix pushing the form in bold and daring new directions. The music, as well as the movement that inspired it, was known as

Stevie Wonder performs live on television in the late 1960s. Influenced by a wide variety of musical styles during this era, he scored several hit singles between 1968 and 1970, including "I Was Made to Love Her," "For Once in My Life," and "Signed, Sealed, Delivered (I'm Yours)."

"psychedelic." Originally used to describe the unfettering of the mind during drug-taking experiences, psychedelia soon came to typify anything that stretched the boundaries of the conventional world. Wonder wanted very much to be a part of this movement and felt very connected to the artists who were driving it forward. "Some of that psychedelic music is really fantastic," he said in Werner's book. "It shows the creativeness of young people. I believe that music is bringing younger people close together. Young people are expressing themselves through music, and that's bringing countries closer together."

One important moment in Wonder's musical journey during this period came when he was in London to appear on the show *Top Gear*. He arrived at the studio early and ran into Jimi Hendrix, the musician who, at age 24, was already the most prominent guitarist of his generation. The two spent some time together and jammed on a few songs. Wonder played drums while Hendrix played guitar with his bassist, Noel

## The Music of the Sixties

Perhaps no other time in music history has produced such a diverse pool of musicians creating at one time. The 1960s were turbulent years, particularly in America, marked by the escalating war in Vietnam, the protests at home, the civil-rights movement, and the space race between the United States and Soviet Union. During these years of change, musicians from America and Britain wrote songs that not only spoke to the times but continue to resonate with modern listeners. Here is a breakdown of some of the most prominent singers and songwriters of the decade:

### THE BEATLES
Because The Beatles' impact on popular music and culture is so massive, it is almost impossible to put it into context today. Paul McCartney, John Lennon, George Harrison, and Ringo Starr began as a simple rock band in Liverpool, England, in the late 1950s but soon went on to change the face of music. The band's diverse musical catalog included such legendary albums as *Please Please Me*, *Rubber Soul*, *Revolver*, and the groundbreaking *Sgt. Pepper's Lonely Hearts Club Band*. When the group split up in 1970, the loss to the music world was keenly felt. Unlike many other 1960s acts, they never performed together again.

### JIMI HENDRIX
Hendrix was a Seattle-born guitarist who had made a name for himself playing the blues in clubs in the South. By the end of the decade, he was being hailed as one of the greatest guitar player in music history. Hendrix's virtuoso style, which fused rock and blues with an array of spaced-out sound effects, was

Redding, backing them up. In Werner's book, a BBC engineer recalled the historic moment:

> Stevie wanted to play the drums to calm down before his interview. Jimi and Noel played along with a bit of "I Was Made to Love Her" for about a minute and a half, and then about another seven minutes of mucking about. It's not that wonderful, but it's one of those legendary things. Stevie Wonder did join with Jimi Hendrix, and it's there on tape."

unique and has never been duplicated. His albums *Are You Experienced?*, *Axis: Bold As Love*, and *Electric Ladyland* have become milestones in rock music. Hendrix died in 1970 at 27 years old, but his legacy continues today.

### THE WHO

Like many of their contemporaries, The Who got their start as a singles band, performing hits like "The Kids Are Alright," "Substitute," and the anthemic "My Generation" in clubs around London. But with the release of *Tommy* in 1969, the band became one of rock's most successful and revered acts. A "rock opera" chronicling the life of a deaf, mute, and blind child who becomes a religious icon due to his mastery of pinball, *Tommy* broke the rules of conventional rock wisdom and catapulted the band to international stardom. The band continued through the 1970s as a major musical force and remains a touring act today, though only two original members, singer Roger Daltrey and guitarist Pete Townshend, remain.

### BOB DYLAN

Born Robert Zimmerman, the singer and poet from Minnesota soon became the voice of a generation. His early protest songs such as "Masters of War," "A Hard Rain's a-Gonna Fall," and "Blowin' in the Wind" became anthems of the protest movement against the Vietnam War. As the decade progressed, Dylan began to experiment with sounds and styles, releasing country-tinged albums (*Nashville Skyline*) and electric-fueled rock albums (*Highway 61 Revisited*) in close proximity. He has continued to record and tour and has remained one of music's most vital creative forces for the past 40 years.

## MUSICAL EXPERIMENTATION

During this period, Wonder became keenly aware of how the times were changing. Although he was churning out hit singles, he was more interested in crafting an entire album of music—not just a collection of 10 or so singles and filler—that was a musical whole. As the decade drew to a close, more and more artists were creating so-called "concept" albums of music, in which each song connected musically or thematically with the other songs on the record. The Beach Boys had crafted *Pet Sounds* in 1966, The Beatles had done *Sgt. Pepper's Lonely Hearts Club Band* in 1967, even Bob Dylan, whose songs Wonder had covered, had scored a tremendous success with his album *Blonde on Blonde* (1966). Wonder began moving in that direction over the next few years, releasing five albums in a three-year period, including the experimental instrumental jazz album *Eivets Rednow* in 1968, the title of which was Wonder's name backward. This album had been released almost secretly, with Wonder's name appearing nowhere on the record sleeve.

In 1970, Wonder released *Signed, Sealed and Delivered,* which continued to show his musical growth. The album yielded several singles, including a cover of The Beatles' "We Can Work It Out." Wonder had long been a fan of the British rock group, and taking on one of their songs was another way for him to step out and explore new musical territory. "When I think of the 60s, I think of two things: I think of Motown and I think of the Beatles," he told Werner.

> Those are the major influences. The Beatles made me feel that I could do some of the ideas that I had. Every time one of their records came out, I wanted to have it, particularly after "Eleanor Rigby." . . . I just dug the effects they got, like echoes and the voice things, the writing, like "For the Benefit of Mr. Kite." I just said, "Why can't I?" I wanted to do something else, go to other places.

Stevie Wonder embraces his bride, Syreeta Wright, a budding Motown songwriter, as they depart Bernette Baptist Church in Detroit, following their wedding ceremony. Wright would have a considerable influence on his musical development in the early 1970s.

## SYREETA WRIGHT

As Wonder's professional career was moving along swiftly, things were also coming together in his personal life. In September 1970, he married Syreeta Wright, a Motown secretary who wanted to become a singer/songwriter and with whom he shared many musical interests. In fact, she helped him write a series of new songs, which Wonder recorded for his 1971 album, *Where I'm Coming From.* As the title suggests, the album was meant to be a statement on his mind-set at the time and represented a bold departure from the established Motown sound. Many people did not know what to make of the album, which included "I Wanna Talk to You," a song about a conversation between a young African American and a racist white man, with Wonder portraying both characters. Regardless of the initial reaction, the album would be the first step in a direction that would lead Stevie Wonder through the most fertile and creative period of his career.

# 7

# Breaking Out

**On May 13, 1971, Stevie Wonder** turned 21 years old and began a fight for creative control over his music. "My contract was made when I was very young," he explained. "And I didn't know the significance of having my own publishing. But I basically wanted to do more. I felt I didn't want to slide into one bag. Music changes, and if you're in the line of change and don't move, you get trampled."

According to Gordy in his autobiography, he received the news that Wonder wanted out from his Motown contract immediately following a twenty-first birthday party Gordy had thrown for the young artist. Arriving at his home in Los Angeles, Gordy found a letter from Wonder's lawyer, demanding that his contract be voided. "I couldn't believe it," he said. "I couldn't believe we could have been together the night before like we were and he [would] not prepare me for something like this. That was not Stevie. But if it was, I was definitely going to tell him about it."

Gordy got in touch with Wonder, who informed him that he had no idea about the letter and that his lawyer had acted without his knowledge. The fact remained, however, that he was looking to get out of his contract. Although Gordy initially balked at the suggestion, he soon realized that Stevie Wonder was a valuable part of Motown that he did not want to lose. As a result, he renegotiated Wonder's contract and gave him complete creative control over his music. It was a bold step for an artist so young, but Gordy believed Wonder had earned it: "Though I had some misgivings . . . I thought of the progression he had made from an eleven-year-old high-pitched singer banging on bongos to a full-voiced vocalist, writer and now producer. I agreed to the creative control. Stevie was ready to fly."

## MUSIC OF MY MIND

Gordy's words proved to be prophetic. Within months of signing his new contract, Wonder was in the studio working on his next record, *Music of My Mind*, which was released in 1972. He had decided to move from Detroit to Jimi Hendrix's Electric Lady Studio in the New York City neighborhood of Greenwich Village, hoping that the change in location would infuse his music with new energy. "I knew I couldn't forever jump up and down and do 'Fingertips,'" he said in an interview with the *New York Times Magazine*.

> I basically wanted to stay with Motown. I've been with them since the beginning, and I felt that I would like to be one of the pioneers of seeing it change, get into a new direction. I knew the company, and I knew the people, and all I had to do was somehow convince Gordy, and part of my convincing had been done when I split. I knew that a lot of the emotions that existed were because of the fact

that I was young, as opposed to looking at me as being a *man*. They were looking at the past, when I was Little Stevie Wonder running up and down the street. So they had another kind of attachment, and it was sort of an insult or hurt to them when I did split, because they could only relate back to the beginning.

Hoping to change everyone's perceptions, Wonder wasted no time in releasing *Music of My Mind*. Following the brashness of *Where I'm Coming From*, *Music of My Mind* was a more focused record, while still charting new musical territory. The album showed a new side to the artist and reflected his introspective and contemplative state of mind. "When I recorded *Music of My Mind*, I didn't have a band then," he said.

I didn't have anybody. I just had myself. I wanted to learn to do this. Plus the time involved, it had taken me longer to explain what I was talking about than I really wanted to take. It wasn't bad, though. Because this is something I really wanted to do. I was very happy with the way it turned out. I wanted to express the way I would have everything sound, the way I would do everything, so I played all the instruments to get that. And basically too because I was using the synthesizer, which is a totally different, whole new world altogether.

By adding the synthesizer—a keyboard-based instrument capable of reproducing a variety of sounds—to his musical arsenal, Wonder was able to broaden his horizons further and continue to develop the style and sound he had been looking for. "The great thing about electronic music is you can make things larger than life," he told Werner. "You can choose colors, and you can make the sounds of an instrument that does not exist."

The radical shift in sound displayed on *Music of My Mind* represented a huge progression not only for Stevie Wonder, but also for the Motown sound. In his autobiography, Berry Gordy recalled his protégé's experimentation:

> I could see him developing a writing and producing style all his own. His lyrics were emotional, poetic and visual;

## The Synthesizer

Although the synthesizer seems like a very modern musical instrument, it has actually been around for more than 100 years. A man named Elisha Gray in 1876 invented the very first synthesizer, which he called the "Musical Telegraph." The invention happened almost by accident. While developing an early version of the telephone, Gray discovered that the same technology could be used to manipulate sound and turn it into music. Over the next 50 years, advances continued to be made in the realm of the synthesizer, but the instrument's sheer size and expense made its access to average musicians limited. As a result, instruments like the electric guitar surged in popularity during the 1940s, while the synthesizer remained confined to labs and workshops.

The man who brought synthesizer technology into its next era was Dr. Robert Moog. A New York-based scientist, Moog developed a workable synthesizer system using transistors that could create electronic music in a studio-based setting. Instantly, musicians wanted to get their hands on this new device. The Monkees were the first band to release an album with a synthesizer with 1967's *Pisces, Aquarius, Capricorn & Jones Ltd.* In 1968, a composer named Wendy Carlos released *Switched-On Bach*, a collection of Bach recordings played on Moog's synthesizer. The album was a smash hit and led to a synthesizer revolution in music. Soon musicians all over the world were adding the instrument to their repertoires and experimenting with the strange and unusual sounds it could produce. Stevie Wonder—as well as bands such as Yes, Rush, Pink Floyd, and Tangerine Dream—began enhancing and expanding their sound by incorporating synthesized musical tones into their recordings. In 1969, the synthesizer had another first when it was used to compose the score for the James Bond film *On Her Majesty's Secret Service.*

Today the synthesizer is a common part of the global music landscape. Many modern artists such as the Rentals, Radiohead, the Beastie Boys, and Air continue to use Moog's technology as a mainstay of their recordings.

his chord patterns intricate and different. His music covered many spectrums—Blues, Pop, Reggae, Classical, Jazz and Stevie himself. For the first time, he began recording in studios other than ours, experimenting with synthesizers and other strange technological apparatus. That

Robert Moog, who designed the best known of the electronic musical synthesizers, makes the final adjustment on his synthesizer prior to a jazz concert at the Museum of Modern Art in New York City, on August 28, 1969. Moog's synthesizers would allow numerous recording artists, including Stevie Wonder, to experiment musically in ways they had never thought possible.

unique texture that was all his own broadened the base of the Motown Sound tremendously.

## TOURING WITH THE ROLLING STONES

Although critics had lauded *Music of My Mind*, Wonder still felt as if he was not reaching audiences in the numbers he believed he could. To a large portion of the record-buying public, Stevie Wonder was only a top-40 artist, a singles-maker from the Motown hit machine. He was eager to prove that his music was capable of reaching a wider range of listeners and sought out a platform from which to do that. It arrived when members of The Rolling Stones invited Wonder and his band, Wonderlove, to join them on the road for their 1972 North American tour. Seeing this as the perfect way to broaden his fan base, he jumped at the chance.

Unfortunately, for all its benefits, touring with the Stones proved to be a major headache. In the early days of the tour, audiences paid little attention during Wonder's set, barely responding to any of his numbers. In addition, the cocaine-fueled decadence of The Rolling Stones was in sharp contrast to Wonder's more straitlaced lifestyle. Oftentimes, in interviews, members of the band would make derogatory remarks about Wonder. "I thought at the very beginning it was going to be good vibes," Wonder said of the tour in a *Rolling Stone* interview from the time. "But you know, I could see we were on two different levels. I never went and got high with them because I don't get high. So maybe that had something to do with it. I don't know. I went a few times to get a drink, some beer or something, but I never really hung out with them."

Although there were many hurdles to overcome, touring with The Rolling Stones proved to be advantageous. One night, Wonder came out to join the band for a rendition of "Uptight (Everything's Alright)," which then segued into the Stones' "Satisfaction." The performance was a smash with the audience, and soon became a regular part of the set. People everywhere began to see Stevie Wonder in a whole new way. "The tour has been good for me," he said later. "At least it lets people know I'm not doing 'Fingertips' anymore."

## TALKING BOOK

Following the tour, Stevie released *Talking Book* (1972), an album that established him as a musical force to be reckoned with. The album also furthered his development as a politically conscious artist. Songs such as "Big Brother," which included the lyrics, "You've killed all our leaders/I don't even have to do nothin' to you/You'll cause your own country to fall," gave Wonder a platform to voice his concerns about the world going on around him. This awareness informed the entire record, as he explained to Werner. "The most interesting thing to me was about civilizations before ours, how advanced people really were, how high they had brought themselves only to bring themselves down because of the missing links, the weak foundations," he reflected.

> So the whole thing crumbled. And that's kind of sad. And it relates to today and what could possibly happen here, very soon. That's basically what "Big Brother" is all about. I speak of the history, the heritage of the violence, or the negativeness of being able to see what's going on with minority people. We don't have to do anything to [the people in power], 'cause they're gonna cause their own country to fall.

Perhaps the centerpiece of *Talking Book* was "Superstition." Originally written for rock musician Jeff Beck, the track was a hard-driving funk-rock number powered by a chugging synthesizer riff and a memorable rise-and-fall horn progression. The main riff was generated by a Hohner clavinet, an electric piano similar to the clavichord, which produces a very distinctive sound. Wonder chose to use this instrument for the lead because, in his words, "it's a funky, dirty, stinky, *nasty* instrument." When Wonder released it as a single, it became his first number-one hit since "Fingertips," proving once and for all that he was not a one-shot child star, but rather an artist who was here to stay.

## INNERVISIONS

Not content to rest on this recent success, Wonder launched into recording his next album almost immediately. He worked around the clock, almost ceaselessly. Being blind, he was not bound by the cycle of day and night in the same way that sighted people are, and so he simply worked until he no longer could. "Stevie is someone who goes into the studio at seven

## Other Famous Synthesizer Players

### KEITH EMERSON
The English-born and classically trained piano player made a name for himself in the late 1960s by playing with a progressive rock group called The Nice. During the band's chaotic stage shows, Emerson would occasionally use knives to wedge down the keys of his synthesizer or play it upside down to thrill the crowd. During the 1970s, Emerson teamed with bassist Greg Lake and drummer Carl Palmer to form Emerson, Lake and Palmer. The trio fused classical music with hard-driving rock to create a sound unlike any other of the era. The band would often use elements of such composers as Bach and Aaron Copland and fuse them with pounding drums and thundering bass. Emerson's piano solos and synth-driven riffs soon made the keyboard the group's lead instrument and helped to create ELP's signature sound.
   Key Albums: *Trilogy*, *Brain Salad Surgery*, *In Concert*

### RICK WAKEMAN
By the time he joined the progressive-rock band Yes in 1971, Wakeman was already an accomplished musician, having sat in on sessions with some of the top artists of the day, including David Bowie and Cat Stevens. But when he teamed with Yes for the *Fragile* album, Wakeman quickly became recognized for his prodigious talent. Similar to Emerson, Wakeman was able to

o'clock at night and comes out at ten o'clock the next morning," a former staff member told Werner.

> Time doesn't mean anything to him while he's creating. He just goes on and on and on. He would stay in the studio even longer if the people who worked with him could keep up with it. Only when we say "Hey, Steve, it's nine o'clock in the morning," then he'd say, "Okay, let me just get these two more tracks down" or something like that.

His intense schedule ultimately had one casualty, his marriage to Syreeta. A little over a year after they were wed, the

blend classical music with rock themes effortlessly, expanding the group's sound dynamically. After leaving the group, he continued to write and record, becoming famous for his incredible concerts, which at one point featured ice skaters live on the stage. Today, Wakeman has rejoined Yes and continues to tour with the group regularly.

Key Albums: *The Six Wives of Henry VIII, Journey to the Centre of the Earth, Fragile* (with Yes)

### HAROLD FALTERMEYER

During the 1980s, Faltermeyer's synth-driven rhythms became the definitive sound for big-budget Hollywood action. His work on 1984's *Beverly Hills Cop* quickly made him a household name. Faltermeyer composed a seven-note theme for the film's hero, Axel Foley, which soon became the main theme of the movie. Titled "Axel F," the song was released as a single and went to number one on the charts. Faltermeyer went on to score a number of hit films during the 1980s, including *The Running Man, Tango & Cash,* and *Top Gun* (his most famous work next to "Axel F"). He currently lives in his native Germany and has expressed interest in returning to soundtrack work.

Key Albums: *Top Gun: Original Motion Picture Soundtrack; Portrait of Harold Faltermeyer: His Greatest Hits; Beverly Hills Cop: Music From the Motion Picture Soundtrack* couple filed for divorce. "We have no negative feelings for each other," he said at the time. "I was too young. Besides, she's a Leo. A Taurus and a Leo are like two sticks of dynamite."

Seven months after heading into the studio, Wonder emerged with *Innervisions* (1973), an album that continued to display his musical growth and his desire to convey political and social messages through his music. Reviewing the album in *Rolling Stone*, critic Lenny Kaye observed:

> *Innervisions* is Wonder's 14th album, his third since fully becoming his own man, and it shows off his talents to luminous advantage. . . . Its tracks are coupled by a hovering mist of subdued faith, of a belief in the essential *rightness* of things. . . . On *Innervisions*, Stevie Wonder proves again that he is one of the vital forces in contemporary music.

*Innervisions* was an album greatly inspired by the urban and social decay that had so much become a part of the post-sixties landscape. Everywhere, cities were growing ever more crowded, crime-ridden, and dirty, and inner-city families were becoming ever more desperate. Singles like "Living for the City," with lyrics such as "His father works some days for fourteen hours/And you can bet he barely makes a dollar/His mother goes to scrub the floors for many/And you'd best believe she hardly gets a penny/Living just enough, just enough for the city," spoke to the hopelessness of life in American cities of the 1970s. "It was a snapshot of a certain part of the reality of life," Wonder told Barney Hoskyns in a 2005 interview for *Uncut*. "'Living for the City' was very real for certain people."

The album also featured the standout track "Higher Ground," which described a world in which soldiers continue to make war as politicians continue to lie. As bleak as the world Wonder painted seemed, the song also contained a message of hope in his repeated chorus of "Gonna keep on tryin'/Till I reach my highest ground/Till I reach my highest ground/No one's gonna

Stevie Wonder performing at the height of his powers in the mid-1970s. During what is now considered his "classic period," he produced numerous hit singles and award-winning concept albums that cemented his reputation as one of the greatest musicians of his generation.

bring me down." According to John Swenson's 1986 biography, *Stevie Wonder*, the musician said of the song,

> "Higher Ground" was a very special song. I wrote it on May 11. I remember the date. I did the whole thing—the words, the music, and recorded the track—in three hours. That's the first time I ever finished a song so fast. It was almost as if I had to get it done. I felt something was going to happen. I didn't know what or when, but I felt something.

In order to promote the album and denote its importance, Wonder planned a press event that was truly unlike any other. Critic Dave Marsh recalled the occasion to Werner:

> They put a whole batch of us on a bus in Times Square and blindfolded us. Then they drove us around for what seemed like a long time—it was probably in the neighborhood of ten minutes, but it felt like half an hour. They pulled up in front of some place and shepherded us off the bus and into a cool, air-conditioned space. Each of us had a guide. Then they played us the record. It was an amazing thing. Totally disorienting. The music had a clarity, a lucidity, and a flat-out power that was greatly increased by the limitation of the visual sense; no distraction, or complete distraction, but in the end, it really focused the whole experience, and *not* only because the music was unforgettable, although of course it was. It was one [heck] of a way to experience "Living for the City" for the first time.

*Innervisions* was embraced not only by critics or one section of people, but by practically the entire record-buying public. The album received rave reviews and today is considered a masterpiece, even among Wonder's stellar albums of the era. In his book *1,000 Recordings to Hear Before You Die*, Tom Moon wrote, "Wriggling through graceful vocal melodies and ad-libs as daring as those from any jazz musician, Wonder speaks truth to power. But he doesn't harangue: Everything comes wrapped in Wonder's resolutely bright, indomitable spirit." Songs on the album proved so popular that musicians as diverse as Barbra Streisand and Frank Sinatra covered them. "Living for the City" inspired sermons, campaigns, and other messages of positivism.

It seemed that Stevie Wonder was now unstoppable. He had recorded three acclaimed albums in a row and had successfully stepped out from the shadows of both Motown and his younger self. Everything was falling into place. Now, a terrible accident would nearly destroy everything he had worked for.

# 8

# Setback and Comeback

**On August 6, 1973, Stevie Wonder** and his cousin John Harris were driving to a concert in Durham, North Carolina. While on the road, they came up behind a large truck carrying a load of logs. The truck was weaving dangerously and Harris, who was driving, decided to pass it. As he began to move around the vehicle, the driver slammed on his brakes and one of the logs broke free. Before anyone realized what had happened, the log smashed through their windshield and collided with Wonder's skull.

The blow knocked the singer unconscious instantly and put him in a coma for the next eight days. His friends and family feared the worst: that he could die or be severely brain-damaged. In Haskins's book, longtime friend Ira Tucker recalled those harrowing days:

> I remember when he got to the hospital in Winston-Salem. Man, I couldn't even recognize him. His head was swollen

up about five times normal size. And nobody could get through to him. I knew that he likes to listen to music really loud and I thought maybe if I shouted in his ear it might reach him. The first time I didn't get any response, but the next day I went back and I got right down in his ear and sang "Higher Ground." His hand was resting on my arm, and after a while, his fingers started going in tune with the song. I said, yeah! Yeeaah! This dude is gonna make it!

Wonder remained in the hospital for close to two weeks, lingering in and out of consciousness during much of that time. When he finally came around, he realized that the brain injury had taken his sense of smell. This was a particularly devastating revelation for Wonder as he was already without one of his five senses. To now have lost two cut him off from the world that much more, and it filled him with dread as to what else he may have lost. He now had to face the terrible possibility that, due to the trauma to his brain, he might not be able to make music the way he once had. Tucker told Haskins:

After he came out of the coma, we brought one of his instruments—I think it was the clavinet—to the hospital. For a while, Stevie just sat there. Didn't do anything with it. You could see he was afraid to touch it, because he didn't know if he still had it in him—he didn't know if he could still play. And then when he finally did touch it! Man, you could just see the happiness spreading all over him. I'll never forget that.

Gradually, Wonder began to recover from his accident. His sense of smell ultimately returned, and his ability to play remained undiminished. And, as his friends soon learned, his wicked sense of humor was just as strong as it had always been. A few days after Wonder had returned home, Berry Gordy's secretary received a call from a man she believed to be Gordy asking her to give Stevie Wonder a check for $50,000. The woman was stunned at the high number and, after a moment, called her boss back to confirm it. Upon hearing what had happened, the real Berry Gordy smiled. He immediately knew that Wonder was up to his old tricks and that everything was going to be all right again.

Following his accident, Wonder found himself to be even more introspective than before. He came to believe that his injury had a purpose and that God had allowed him to survive in order to fulfill a higher calling. "The only thing I know is that I was unconscious," he said later of the days following his accident, "and that for a few days I was definitely in a much better spiritual place that made me aware of a lot of things that concern my life and my future and what I have to do to reach another higher ground. This is like my second chance for life, to do something or to do more and to face the fact that I am alive."

## COMING BACK

A few months into his recovery, Wonder was asked by friends of the British pop sensation Elton John to come to Boston to attend a show, an invitation he was pleased to accept. He was flown out on John's private jet and met with the singer/pianist backstage before the show. As John was about to perform his encore, he made an announcement to the crowd. "A friend of mine is here," he told the 18,000-strong audience. "He was badly hurt in an accident some time ago." That was as far as he got. Instantly the crowd realized whom he was referring to and rose to their feet, cheering and clapping furiously. Wonder then took the stage and joined in on a rendition of "Honky Tonk Women," a bluesy, piano-driven riff on The Rolling Stones' song, which then segued into "Superstition." If there had been any doubt beforehand, there could be no mistaking it now: Stevie Wonder was back.

With the accident and injury firmly in his past, Wonder threw himself back into recording with a renewed sense of

**Stevie Wonder, right, is joined by Alice Cooper after he won four Grammys at the Sixteenth annual Grammy Awards, held on March 2, 1974, in Los Angeles, California. Cooper was one of the presenters.**

excitement and passion. Although he worked around the clock as usual, Wonder did take a break in March 1974 to attend the Grammy Awards. He had been nominated for six of them, the most nominations any artist had received up to that point. At the end of the night, Wonder went home with four awards, including Album of the Year for *Innervisions.* In accepting the awards, Wonder was genuinely humbled. "Never did I think I would receive a Grammy," he said in Haskins's book. "My only goal and dream was to touch and know how a Grammy looked. I guess God didn't let me touch just one. He let me touch four."

In April 1974, shortly after his Grammy victory, Wonder performed his first live concert since the accident. The sold-out crowd at Madison Square Garden welcomed him back with a roar of approval. Describing the scene, one journalist wrote in *Time*:

> Sporting a mustache and his familiar dark glasses, he pointed toward heaven, then to his forehead and finally cut loose with a survivor's smile. From the balcony, loges and floor of the Garden came a roar—20,000 voices strong—of adulation, welcome and animal joy.... It was fine to hear a voice so long addicted to sweet soul now revel in husky, emotive blues growls. The pulsating climax came with an almost symphonic version of his "Living [for] the City," a black odyssey that begins in Mississippi and ends with the arrest of an innocent youth in New York.... Wonder topped that off by bringing out three fellow blacks—Sly Stone, Eddie Kendricks and Roberta Flack— for a reprise of "Superstition" and a rollicking, hand-clapping, ear piercing finale....

## The Grammys

Short for "Gramophone," the Grammy Award is music's most prestigious prize, the equivalent of Hollywood's Academy Award. The Grammy is presented each year to recognize outstanding achievements in the world of music. The awards are presented by the National Academy of Recording Arts and Sciences, which was founded in 1957. Two years later, the first awards ceremony was held at the Beverly Hilton in Los Angeles. At first, the Grammys were not shown on TV. A TV special titled *The Best on Record*, which showed highlights of the awards ceremonies, would air instead.

Sitting up there onstage, his head bobbing and weaving sightlessly as though trying to tune in on some private radar of the mind, he recalls no one so much as his old idol . . . Ray Charles.

## FULFILLINGNESS' FIRST FINALE

Wonder's next album was released July 22, 1974, and was cryptically titled *Fulfillingness' First Finale*. Some people did not know what to make of the album's name, but Wonder felt it was appropriate. "*Fulfillingness*' was just me working the word," he said to Gail Mitchell in a 2004 interview. "The idea of fulfilling and fulfilling is like a female. The other part of that title, 'the first finale,' was sort of referencing an ending of the period after *Music of My Mind* and these three albums."

In contrast to *Innervisions*, the tone of *Fulfillingness' First Finale* was darker and more somber, perhaps as a result of Wonder's reflective state of mind following the accident. Even Wonder himself recognized that the record reflected a shift in tone. "I think *Fulfillingness*' was a good album," he told Hoskyns, "but I don't know if it was equal to *Innervisions*, to be honest with you. It was different. In one sense, it was rawer." Regardless, *Fulfillingness' First Finale* was another success, rocketing to number one on the charts and generating hit singles with "You Haven't Done Nothin'" and "Boogie on Reggae Woman." In total, the album earned him four Grammys, including his second for Album of the Year. Wonder's dominance of both the charts and the awards led to a now-famous moment in 1976 when Paul Simon, accepting his Album of the Year award for *Still Crazy After All These Years*, jokingly thanked Stevie for not releasing an album in the previous year.

The world had now embraced Stevie Wonder fully, but he was only just getting started. After touring in support of *Fulfillingness' First Finale*, the singer headed back into the studio yet again. Perhaps driven by the industry's labeling of him as a "soul" singer, Wonder was determined to create an album that transcended genres and defied categorization. He said in Haskins's book:

> I don't like it when one is put into a category of music, so that when he ventures into some other kind of music the press or the public has a hard time relating to it. It seems that every person is put into a certain bag. Being an artist is not being limited to one kind of music. For instance, soul music was derived from gospel and early rhythm and blues. In my mind, soul means feeling. When a person is categorized as a soul artist because of his color, I don't

## Notable Grammy Winners

Although Stevie Wonder is famous for taking home multiple Grammys, these artists have also filled their shelves with several of the awards.

### GEORG SOLTI

The name might not be familiar to you, but Georg Solti is the most accomplished Grammy winner in the history of the awards. Before his death in 1997, the Hungarian-born classical composer had amassed 31 Grammys, with a Lifetime Achievement Award bringing the number to 32. And he was nominated more than 70 times.

### ALISON KRAUSS

A bluegrass composer, songwriter, and performer, Krauss has taken home 26 Grammys, the most for any female artist in the history of the awards. She has won Grammys for her work with her band, Union Station, as well as for her work as a record producer. In 2007, Krauss teamed with former Led Zeppelin frontman Robert Plant for the album *Raising Sand*, which took home five Grammys, including Album of the Year.

### U2

With 125 million albums sold, this Irish foursome is unquestionably the most successful and accomplished band of all time. The band has taken home 22 Grammys since winning its first for its 1987 album, *The Joshua Tree*, the most for any band in history, including The Beatles.

like it. True artistry is about variety, the real spice of an artist's life.

So determined was Wonder to create an album that went beyond conventional labels that he spent two years working on it. As 1975 came and went, it marked the first calendar year in which Wonder had not released an album since he began recording music 13 years earlier. Ever the perfectionist, he worked tirelessly on each song until he felt it was just right, sometimes spending 48 hours in a row in the studio. People began to wonder if this new album would ever be released, which prompted Wonder to start wearing a custommade T-shirt that read "We're Almost Finished." Around the Motown offices, staffers took Wonder's cue and began wearing shirts of their own with the slogan "Stevie's Almost Ready."

Also during this time, Wonder fell in love with a woman named Yolanda Simmons, a secretary and bookkeeper in his organization. Although they were not married, they moved in together; in April 1975, their daughter Aisha Zakia was born.

### SONGS IN THE KEY OF LIFE

When Wonder's new album was finally released in September 1976, it comprised two LPs and one bonus EP (extended play). Titled *Songs in the Key of Life*, the oversized album was a wideranging, expansive collection covering a wide variety of music, ranging from jazz and the blues to funk and rock, with a bit of classical thrown in for good measure. The lyrics covered such topics as racism, war, poverty, and family life. "Village Ghetto Land" addressed life in the inner cities, while "Have a Talk With God" focused on religion seeing one through hard times, and the upbeat "Isn't She Lovely" was written in tribute to Aisha. "It happened simply because I had all those songs," said Wonder of the album's expansive content. "I felt that all of them were, again, snapshots of a time and a place and an emotion that fit together very well. I'm very conscious of the

**Stevie Wonder** *(right)* **and his daughter Aisha, with clowns at the Ringling Bros., Barnum & Bailey Circus backstage at Madison Square Garden in New York City, on March 27, 1978. Wonder wrote his hit single "Isn't She Lovely" for his daughter when she was a newborn.**

flow of the music on an album and that whole deal, because I'm listening objectively as a person."

While audiences embraced the album feverishly, sending it straight to number one on the charts for 14 weeks, critics' praise was slightly more measured. While admiring the album's variety, Vince Aletti wrote in *Rolling Stone* that the album "has no focus or coherence. The eclecticism is rich and welcome, but the overall effect is haphazard, turning what might have been a stunning, exotic feast into a hastily organized potluck supper."

In spite of what some critics had to say, *Songs in the Key of Life* grew to become almost unanimously recognized as not only one of Wonder's finest achievements, but also one of the greatest albums of all time in *any* genre. Its success led Gordy to sign Wonder to a new contract, guaranteeing him $13 million over seven years. At the time, it was the largest contract in the history of the music business. When the Grammy Awards rolled around in 1977, Wonder found himself with seven nominations, taking home three including Album of the Year. Wonder accepted his Grammy via a satellite connection from Nigeria.

Wonder had begun traveling to Africa in 1975 and had grown fond of the continent and its people. He had also grown keenly aware of the poverty, hunger, and disease that affected many Africans. Realizing his potential to affect great change, he began making regular visits to the continent and donating large sums of his fortune to various causes in the region. After five successful albums in a row, culminating in what many considered to be his masterpiece, Stevie Wonder was ready to answer a higher calling.

# 9

# A Shift in Focus

**After a creative burst that saw** him through the decade, Wonder closed out the 1970s rather quietly. After 1976, he released only one album, 1979's *Journey Through the Secret Life of Plants*. A soundtrack to the documentary film *The Secret Life of Plants*, *Journey* was a double album comprised mostly of instrumentals and proved to be confusing for many listeners, particularly following the varied masterwork of *Songs in the Key of Life*. Critics were not kind. Ken Tucker, writing in *Rolling Stone*, called the album "bloated" and observed that "plucking the exhilarating moments from *Journey through the Secret Life of Plants* is a harrowing, highly subjective task. One person's nectar is another's Karo syrup, and the stamens of Wonder's Plants are bursting with both." Even the ever-loyal Gordy had his doubts. "When I first heard it," he wrote in his autobiography, "I had the sinking feeling it might not be the smash we so desperately needed from Stevie." So concerned was he that Gordy lowered the number of advance pressings. "And still," he noted, "that turned out to be around nine hundred thousand too many."

*Journey Through the Secret Life of Plants* disappeared quickly, failing to notch any Grammy Awards or nominations, a first for Wonder in some time. Today, while the quality of its musical content is still debatable, the album is considered to be an important milestone in Wonder's ever-evolving sound. Even Wonder himself looks at the album as an achievement. "It was not a success on the charts, but I'd like to think of it as an accomplishment for me," he told Steve Morse for the *Boston Globe*. "I had wanted for a long time to show that a blind person could write music that was somewhat visual. It was a success in terms of something that was challenging. And that's what matters to me."

In 1980, Wonder returned with his first official album in four years, *Hotter Than July*. To most, it represented a return to form, as highlighted by the single "Master Blaster (Jammin')," a reggae-infused number inspired by the legendary Jamaican performer Bob Marley.

### BRANCHING OUT

As the eighties progressed, Wonder slowed his pace considerably. He turned his attention toward humanitarian causes and spending more time with his family. "Music and life go in cycles," he told Divina Infusino in an interview with the *San Diego Union*. "Music takes a different position in your life at different times. If you're doing a lot of things, then that takes away from your creative time."

Among the causes Wonder was passionate about was the designation of Martin Luther King Jr.'s birthday as a national holiday. Wonder's involvement with the movement to recognize the slain civil-rights leader began with the single "Happy Birthday" from *Hotter Than July*, and continued when he hosted the 1981 Rally For Peace press conference, which championed the holiday. In 1983, President Ronald Reagan signed the day into law, marking the third Monday of January as Martin Luther King Jr. Day. "You can assassinate the man, but you can't kill the values," Wonder said at the time. "I knew Reagan would sign the bill."

In 1982, Wonder released *Stevie Wonder's Original Musiquarium*, a greatest-hits collection that also featured four new songs. That same year, he teamed up with Paul McCartney, himself a musical icon as a former member of The Beatles, to record the song "Ebony and Ivory." The single uses the metaphor of black and white keys on a piano to touch on issues of racial harmony and was another hit for Wonder. Released in the spring of 1982, the single spent seven weeks at number one on the charts. Some critics derided the song as simplistic and saccharine, with *Blender* naming it one of their "50 Worst Songs of All Time," but Wonder explained that the song's simplicity is key to conveying its message. "Lots of times when things are said very clearly it is almost like speaking in the mind of a child," he told Werner. "I felt that for whatever significance we both have, both in multi-colored, multi-racial society, we're all so many different colors and cultures, it would be good for us to sing something like that."

Wonder spent much of the following year immersed in a new album, which was to be called *People Move Human Plays* and was slated for release in late 1983. The album, however, was

## IN HIS OWN WORDS...

In the 1980s, Stevie Wonder took up many humanitarian causes, including the fight against the repressive system of apartheid in South Africa:

I wanted to speak out, and do it in a way where people will feel the rhythm of it, but also get the message across, in a peaceful way that's also strong. And the message to the people of South Africa is, "Hold on tight, the whole world is with us, freedom is coming." I want to participate in anything else that's going to be meaningful to the people there.

**Stevie Wonder joins Paul McCartney to sing their hit "Ebony and Ivory" as they perform onstage together for the first time at the Forum in California, on November 29, 1989.**

canceled for unknown reasons and the songs have yet to surface. The only dose of Stevie Wonder audiences received that year was his appearance on the sketch comedy show *Saturday Night Live*. As host and musical guest, Wonder impressed viewers with his ability to poke fun at himself, most notably in a skit with comedian Eddie Murphy, in which Murphy imitated the singer and joked about his blindness. Talking to Steve Morse for the *Boston Globe*, Wonder looked back at the experience fondly. "Maybe we'll do that again," he said. "Because that was another thing about me that people didn't know I could do. Yeah, I can laugh at myself, have fun and get crazy.

Sometimes there's this image of Stevie Wonder as just being this blind, spiritual man whose eyes are in his mind."

In 1984, Wonder finally released new music, in the form of the soundtrack for the Gene Wilder film *The Woman in Red*. Wonder produced the record and performed most of the tracks on it. Wilder, who had been interested in having Wonder perform on the soundtrack for the film, asked Dionne Warwick contact the singer. "Three days later he'd written two songs and played them over the phone to me," Wilder told Werner. "Then he wrote one more, and I thought that was it. I went to France to relax for a week. Then I got a call at two A.M. It was Dionne saying Stevie wanted to write more." The album was released in August 1984 and spawned the hit single "I Just Called to Say I Love You," which spent three weeks atop the U.S. charts and six weeks at number one in the United Kingdom.

On the heels of the success of "I Just Called to Say I Love You," his most popular single since his 1970s heyday, Wonder released his 1985 album, *In Square Circle*, his first official release in half a decade. The album was very much a reflection of the musical styles of the eighties, featuring heavy use of keyboards and slick, electronic production. The album's first single, "Part Time Lover," became another smash for Wonder, reaching number one on the pop, R&B, dance, and adult contemporary charts. This made Wonder the first artist ever to achieve such simultaneous success. In later interviews, Wonder would say that, in spite of its tremendous reception, he had had higher hopes for *In Square Circle*. "I wanted it to be a double album," he said. "People only heard half of what was supposed to be there. But Motown said that with the economic situation the way it is, people aren't buying double albums."

## RESURGENCE

Economics and single albums aside, the success of *In Square Circle* coupled with "I Just Called to Say I Love You" marked a revival in interest in Stevie Wonder. On March 25, 1985, he

## Apartheid

One of the standout tracks on *In Square Circle* is "It's Wrong (Apartheid)," a song that speaks to Wonder's continued interest in political issues. This particular song deals with the issue of apartheid, a legal system in South Africa that maintained complete separation of people by race from 1948 until 1994. Wonder was a strong opponent of apartheid and spoke out against it often. "One of the stupidest things that exists in the world is the oppression of people," he said. "I'll tell people [in concert] that in some parts of the world, a gathering like the audience that will be attending my show would be outlawed.

President Nelson Mandela hugs Stevie Wonder at Mandela's residence in Pretoria, South Africa, on February 6, 1996. During Mandela's long imprisonment, Wonder spoke out on behalf of Mandela and against South Africa's brutal policy of apartheid.

Of course, I'm talking about South Africa and Apartheid. It's hard to believe that such a thing is going on in 1986, but it is."

Wonder was also a vocal supporter of Nelson Mandela, a famed anti-apartheid activist who had been in a South African prison since the early 1960s. During his time in jail, Mandela had become the face and voice of the antiapartheid movement, and "Free Nelson Mandela" soon became an oft-repeated slogan by activists, including Wonder. The song "It's Wrong (Apartheid)" on *In Square Circle* was an important one for Wonder. "I wanted to speak out, and do it in a way where people will feel the rhythm of it, but also get the message across, in a peaceful way that's also strong," he said to Robert Palmer in the *New York Times*. "And the message to the people of

*(continues)*

*(continued)*

South Africa is, 'Hold on tight, the whole world is with us, freedom is coming.' I want to participate in anything else that's going to be meaningful to the people there."

When he received the Academy Award for "I Just Called to Say I Love You," Wonder accepted the award in Mandela's name, a move that resulted in his music being instantly banned in South Africa. Wonder had no objections: "If my being banned means people will be free, ban me mega-times."

Nelson Mandela was freed from prison in 1990 and became South Africa's first black president in 1994, at which point apartheid was eradicated, signifying victory for Mandela, South Africans, and the tireless work of activists like Stevie Wonder.

accepted the Academy Award for Best Original Song for "I Just Called to Say I Love You." The following year he appeared on the hit television series *The Cosby Show* in an episode that featured the Huxtable family meeting the artist and performing with him in his studio. One scene in particular showcased Wonder's generational appeal. When the Huxtable kids realize they are going to have a chance to meet Wonder, they run from the room dancing and singing "I Just Called to Say I Love You." Claire, the mother, pretends to be unfazed until the children are out of sight, then leaps up excitedly and sings "Isn't She Lovely" before exiting. Finally, the father (played by Bill Cosby), who has feigned disinterest the entire time, waits until he is alone, then enthusiastically sings a few bars of "Livin' for the City."

Wonder also became involved in the campaign against drunken driving, composing the song "Don't Drive Drunk" and recording a video that also served as a public-service announcement. He also lent his image to a poster that found its way into 16,000 high schools and featured the phrase, "Before I ride with a drunk, I'll drive myself."

Wonder quickly capitalized on his success by releasing *Characters* in 1987. The album produced two singles, "You Will Know" and "Skeletons," the latter of which was featured in the hit action film *Die Hard* the following year. Wonder saw the album as an embodiment of his views on the world and rec-

## We Are the World

In 1985, Stevie Wonder joined with some of the most celebrated artists of the period, including Lionel Richie, Billy Joel, Tina Turner, and Bruce Springsteen, to record "We Are the World." The single, produced by Michael Jackson and Quincy Jones, was written and recorded in order to help relieve famine and disease in Africa, specifically Ethiopia, a country crippled by famine as a result of drought and civil war.

The single was attributed to "USA for Africa," which stood for "United Support of Artists for Africa," and was a tremendous success. Released simultaneously on 5,000 radio stations around the country, the song went to number one around the world and quickly became a pop-culture phenomenon.

"We Are the World" also had its share of detractors, who felt the entire event was simply a showcase for the singers and not about helping anyone. Writing in *Higher Ground*, Werner noted:

> While no one could question the cause, the media coverage meshed all too easily with the mid-eighties obsession with the rich and famous. The massive satellite linkup enabled a giant sing-along involving Stevie, Aretha [Franklin], Paul McCartney, Johnny Cash, Whitney Houston, Diana Ross, Michael Jackson and Jackson's date Liz Taylor. The televised images of the glitterati did nothing to lessen the disquieting sense that the event was really *about* the celebrities.

Nevertheless, the single helped to raise more than $44 million in relief money for Africa and helped to inspire other cause-related singles, including "That's What Friends Are For," a song performed by Dionne Warwick and Friends (which included Wonder). Released in late 1985, that song went to number one in January 1986 and became the top-selling single of that year. It was recorded as a benefit for American Foundation for AIDS Research and raised more than $3 million for that cause.

ognized that, while his beliefs might not always be popular, he would not stop expressing them. "I can't really worry about it," he said in an interview with *Jet*. "I wouldn't ever say anything to insult anybody. But, I will express how I feel. I really do feel that love is the only way we're going to come together."

Wonder had planned on continuing the message of *Characters* by releasing *Characters II* in October 1988. That follow-up album, however, never came to be, and instead, he closed out the decade with a duet with singer Julio Iglesias called "My Love," which hit the charts in both the United States and Europe. The following year, he was inducted into the Rock and Roll Hall of Fame. Although he was only 38 years old at the time, he had been recording so long that he fit well within the 25-year period required for induction.

While the 1980s were not as prolific musically as the previous decade had been, Wonder had been able to shift his focus from tireless creation to activism and political action. He also slowed his pace in order to spend more time with his family. At that point, he had three children, Aisha, Keita, and a son, Mumtaz, whom he had with vocalist Melody McCulley. "I try to be a real father to my kids instead of some kind of star," he said. "I try to make the time I spend with them quality time."

## MOVING INTO THE 1990s

Although eight years would pass between the release of *Characters* and his next studio album, Wonder did not take that time to rest and count his earnings. He remained very busy, recording the soundtrack to Spike Lee's 1991 film *Jungle Fever*. The movie, about an African-American architect who enters into an affair with a white secretary, was successful, and the soundtrack yielded a hit single with "Jungle Fever."

In 1992, Wonder traveled to Ghana, a country on Africa's Ivory Coast, to perform at Pana-Fest, the nation's first-ever music festival. Wonder's time in the country was incredibly influential on him. "I went there in the summer of '92 and

I'd only been there for 18 hours when I decided I'd eventually move there permanently," he told Pete Lewis in an interview for *Blues & Soul.*

> So, when I was invited back again by the President to stay at the Government house, I wrote about 40 songs within that month-and-a-half stay. You know, I was a little bit away from the phone ringing and just in a great situation, where I could let the gift of God work and give me ideas and inspiration to come up with some songs that I feel good about.

Of the 40 songs that Wonder composed during that trip, 13 came together to form *Conversation Peace,* his first official studio album since *Characters.* Released in the spring of 1995, the album was largely well received by critics, though some lamented that the record did not represent a return to the singer's *Songs in the Key of Life* heyday. "As fluff-covered talents go, this one is surprisingly flavourful," wrote Jim Irvin in *Mojo.*

> *Conversation Peace* may be irritating when Wonder settles for the kind of crunch 'n' squeak dance groove nowadays available by the yard, and might exasperate when he resorts to half-hearted hip hop moves, but the melodies are reliably creamy and intoxicating. A good Stevie Wonder tune is still like having Baileys poured in your ear.

In addition to wanting to hear the album itself, people were interested in why it took so long for Wonder, who once churned out a record a year, to release it. "Unlike some have suggested, no writers block has happened—basically what I've done is just allow me the time to experience life," he told Lewis.

> As much as this is a business that I am in, I make it my business to not make it *such* a business that I can not do

the natural process! While economically it is a great thing to have a record out every year-and-a-half, and there are definite draw-backs if you don't ... when you're given the gift of music you must also allow yourself to replenish and experience the things you have to do in life. I mean, the many composers of hundreds of years ago didn't have records out every year-and-a-half! So I don't feel funny about the time that it takes me at all!

*Conversation Peace* was released in a time when soul and R&B were on the wane and so-called gangsta rap ruled the urban charts. Fueled by such artists as Notorious B.I.G., Snoop Doggy Dogg, and Tupac Shakur, gangsta rap spoke of the violent, turbulent, and crime-ridden life on the streets of America's inner cities and painted a grim picture for the rest of the country. While many people, including Spike Lee, criticized the genre for its controversial views on race, class, and gender, Wonder came to its defense, feeling that the rap artists were, in a sense, conveying their own political message through their music, just as he was. "I see a lot of rappers as modern-day griots," he told Lewis.

As you know, the griots were the ancient story-tellers of the African villages and it is no different today. Unfortunately there's a lot of pain within the hearts of young people, and I know as a man of 44 that I'm glad I was not raised in this time. All of which says, or shows, that we have not done a really great job, and we as older adults are gonna have to change that, and I think that's a responsibility of everyone throughout the world! There is opportunity for change, and I think that we can make those changes. If not, I do believe that, in the spiritual realm, the power of God along with nature will change it, whether it be through natural disaster, whatever. . . . You know, people are gonna have to wake up!

On October 16, 1995, Wonder attended the Million Man March, a gathering of African-American men from across the United States held in Washington, D.C. The event was designed to forge a sense of unity among African-American men and help to create a more positive and proactive mindset in the furthering of African-American family and cultural values. Wonder was among the speakers that day.

"I cannot visually see you, but ... I can feel your presence. . . . I'm here for every poor man born in the ghetto, every middle class [man] born in the middle class, and for every rich man, to say that no matter where we might be in class, we are all one people," he told the crowd.

> Staring right at 2000 A.D., as if mankind's atrocities to man [have] no history, but [in] just a glance at life in 2000 B.C., we can find traces of man's inhumanity to man. There goes history. All for one and one for all. There's no way unless we heed the call. Me for you, you for me. There's no chance of world salvation unless the conversation speaks.

Although he continued to be involved in social causes, Wonder also remained active as a performer. Two particular standout performances of the decade included his rendition of John Lennon's "Imagine" at the 1996 Olympic Games in Atlanta, Georgia, and when he joined the cast of the Broadway hit *Rent* for "Seasons of Love," which was included on the original cast recording.

## HELPING THE BLIND

Also in 1995, Wonder branched out from beyond the realm of music to create a children's book called *Little Stevie Wonder in Places Under the Sun*. The book uses Braille, printed words, and pictures to tell a story of Wonder's trip to Japan with his friends. The book also included a Braille alphabet in order to teach the language to children with sight. For the audio recording, his son, Mumtaz, provided the voice of Little Stevie Wonder.

In May 1997, Wonder and the company Systems, Applications, and Products in Data Processing, Inc. (SAP) came together to create the SAP/Stevie Wonder Vision Awards. SAP is a global enterprise designed to create technology that allows blind and disabled people to use their abilities. The Vision Award is a cash prize given to a person, product, or organization that works toward creating a better working environment for disabled people. The inaugural winning product was the Kurzweil 1000, a reading system that converts the printed word into speech. In presenting the award, Wonder gave the audience a dose of his usual good humor and characteristic wit: "The real reason I got involved in this whole thing was because, I figure, about two years from now, I'd like to be driving!"

In 1999, he met with doctors at the Wilmer Eye Institute at the Johns Hopkins University Medical Center to discuss an experimental surgery that could have restored his sight. Known as intraocular retinal prosthesis (IRP), the procedure involved implanting a computer chip in the retina. Using electrical stimulation, some patients were able to regain at least a small portion of their vision. Unfortunately, Wonder's particular form of blindness was not the ideal condition for the treatment, and the most promising candidates were ones who initially had full vision. Although as of this writing the surgery remains experimental, some advances have been made. Wonder has taken the diagnosis in stride and remains positive regardless:

I think that there is God's divine plan and as much as it was a misfortune for me to end up . . . blind, I don't feel that I have missed out on too much in life . . . there are things that I sometimes think I've seen even more vividly than people [who] can see, and I think that all of us—whether we see or not—we use a lot of what we hear as our first and sometimes lasting impressions.

Stevie Wonder closed out the twentieth century in grand fashion on December 5, 1999, by becoming the youngest-ever recipient of the Kennedy Center Honors, an annual honor given to select individuals who have excelled in the performing arts. The red-carpet event featured a number of celebrity guests, including Bill Cosby, Coretta Scott King, and fellow honoree Sean Connery, as well as a musical performance from Smokey Robinson, whose band-mate Ronnie White, who had died from leukemia in 1995, first brought Wonder to Motown's attention. Accepting the honor, Wonder was humbled. "I'm very, very thankful," he said. "I thank God for this blessing. It's just a beginning to what I can do to encourage and to inspire throughout the next millennium. But I'm also very happy as well that the legacy of what John F. Kennedy had a vision for has lasted so long."

# 10

# A Bright Future

**As the twenty-first century arrived,** Stevie Wonder's place in music history was secure. Musicians everywhere cited him as an influence, and a new generation of artists who had grown up on his music were now creating albums of their own and crediting Wonder for his inspiration. British soul singer Beverley Knight described Stevie Wonder's continued impact in the London *Guardian*:

> My generation, the generation below me, the generation that's older than me—Stevie Wonder has influenced the lot of us. He's someone we keep seeing reborn, in a way, through other artists. Albums like *Hotter Than July*, *Songs in the Key of Life* and [*Innervisions*] don't date, they don't age, they're not things you get tired of, and they still hold up. If the music can

## Artists Who Have Covered Stevie Wonder's Music

Stevie Wonder's music has been sampled and remade by artists covering every genre. Here are just a few examples of the wide appeal of Wonder's output.

### PUBLIC ENEMY
The influential Long Island rap group sampled "Livin' for the City" on their song "Black Steel in the Hour of Chaos" on their 1988 album, *It Takes a Nation of Millions to Hold Us Back*.

### WILL SMITH
For his title song from the 1999 film *Wild Wild West*, the rapper-turned-actor lifted a sample from Wonder's "I Wish."

### THE JACKSON 5
Before he became the King of Pop, Michael Jackson fronted this hit-making pop band that offered its own interpretation of Wonder's "My Cherie Amour."

### STEVIE RAY VAUGHAN & DOUBLE TROUBLE
The great blues guitarist tore through a blistering rendition of "Superstition" on his 1986 live album, *Live Alive*. Five years after Vaughan's death, Wonder paid tribute to him with the song "Stevie Ray Blues."

### COOLIO
The 1995 film *Dangerous Minds* featured the song "Gangsta's Paradise," which lifted the main riff from Wonder's *Songs in the Key of Life* cut "Pastime Paradise." Technically, Wonder has also been covered by Weird Al Yankovic, since the parody artist recorded a mock version of "Gangsta's Paradise" titled "Amish Paradise."

### FRANK SINATRA
A testament to the wide range of Wonder's appeal is the fact that Frank Sinatra, one of the most revered singers of his, or any other, era, chose to cover "You Are the Sunshine of My Life" on his 1974 album *Some Nice Things I've Missed*.

### ELTON JOHN
A staunch admirer of Wonder's music, the flamboyant British singer/song-writer offered his take on "Signed, Sealed, Delivered (I'm Yours)" for a 1994 album.

speak, and continue to speak, and continue to have the ripple effect it clearly has done—and he's still out on the road doing what he does—then that's all I need to know.

Although he did not release any new albums during the first five years of the new century, Wonder remained a very public presence. In 2000, Motown rereleased four of his biggest albums, *Music of My Mind, Talking Book, Innervisions,* and *Fulfillingness' First Finale,* fully remastered in new packages with extensive liner notes, as a way to introduce the artist to a whole new generation of listeners. According to Joel Selvin, writing for the *San Francisco Chronicle,* the albums "still gleam, almost 30 years after they were first released, with the extraordinary confidence, the amazing gifts, the incredible music that was inside this young man."

Two years later, in 2002, Wonder met with British inventor Richard Smith, who was developing an electronic harmonica. After meeting with Smith, Wonder backed the invention, giving it his seal of approval. Smith's company, Harmonix, now distributes the instruments all over the world. Later that year, Wonder also performed at the opening ceremonies of the 2002 Paralympics in Salt Lake City. The Paralympics run following the closing ceremonies of the Olympic Games and feature sporting events and competitions for athletes with disabilities. That same year, he also received the Sammy Cahn Lifetime Achievement Award, presented by Joan Osborne at a ceremony for the Songwriters Hall of Fame in New York City.

In 2005, Wonder performed at the American portion of the Live 8 concerts. Designed to celebrate the twentieth anniversary of the Live Aid benefit concert, as well as to raise awareness about aid to Africa and fairer trade rules, the concert was a massive, global event featuring 10 concerts on four continents. Wonder performed in Philadelphia and assembled a setlist of his best-known songs, including "Master Blaster (Jammin')," "Signed, Sealed, Delivered (I'm Yours)," and "Superstition."

## *A TIME TO LOVE*

In October of that year, Wonder released *A Time to Love*, his first new album in 10 years. The album was eagerly anticipated, so much so that some fans and industry professionals expressed frustration at the delay. Talking to Johnnie L. Roberts for *Newsweek*, Wonder sympathized with them. "I can understand that," he said.

> But as much as it may cause frustration, hopefully the consequences will be they are going to be happier with the album they will get than the one they might have got sooner.... However long it will take, I'm giving the very best I can. I have a vision, and I won't settle for less.... Probably the most important thing is if I've been working on songs for 10 years, what's a couple more months?

The album was obviously a labor of love for Wonder. "You set a goal in your mind," he told Alan Light in an interview for the *New York Times*, "and you say, O.K., this is what these songs need to have, this project needs to have, and you don't really settle for anything less than that."

For the recording, Wonder attempted to return to a freer, more organic sound by using acoustic instruments instead of the electronic, preprogrammed sounds he had employed during the 1980s and 1990s. He even picked up his drumsticks for the first time in decades. "There were always people going, 'Hey, Stevie, why don't you play drums like you did on *Innervisions*?'" he told Light. "And I'd say, 'Man, that was back then, leave me alone!' But I went back and listened, and I said, 'You know what? They've got a point.'"

*A Time to Love* featured a number of guest singers, including Bonnie Raitt, India.Arie, and Prince. Even former Beatle and Wonder's "Ebony and Ivory" collaborator Paul McCartney contributed guitar parts to the album's title track. But perhaps the CD's most rewarding cuts were the songs "Positivity" and

"How Will I Know?" *A Time to Love* was Wonder's take on many of the troubles in the world of 2005 and his belief that it was vital to think about how we treat one another. "There's a lot of things happening that show us that this, right now, is a time to love," he told *People*. "Terrorism, Iraq. Even the weather is crazy right now. I just think that we have to hold straight to our commitment to love through all the storms." Although many of the songs had been written years earlier, Wonder updated them and reshaped them to fit into the themes of today's world. An example is the track "Shelter from the Rain," which he dedicated to the victims of Hurricane Katrina. The proceeds from the song were used to aid in disaster relief for the city of New Orleans, which had been devastated by the storm in August 2005. The song, however, had not been inspired by the destructive storm. "I wrote it a while back, because I was dealing with something myself," he told Chris Willman for *Entertainment Weekly*.

> My brother was terminally ill, and shortly after that, I found out my first wife, Syreeta, was as well. When they were going through their last days, I was inspired to write a song. It was the only medicine for the wounds and pain that I felt in my heart. I never imagined I would be singing something like that to Syreeta. I wanted to take that song and—because of what it did for me, when God gave it to me—give it to those people that survived Hurricane Katrina that needed to be encouraged. Because there are things that are a lot bigger than life, even, and it's hard for us to really even conceive how big that is.

During this period, Wonder never stopped working for various causes around the world. Shortly before the release of *A Time to Love*, Wonder performed at golfer Tiger Woods's "Tiger Jam" concert, a benefit for the Tiger Woods Foundation that has raised more than $10 million for various charities over

**Stevie Wonder performs in support of his "A Wonder Summer's Night Dream Tour 2007" to a sold-out crowd at the Sleep Train Pavilion in Concord, California, on August 26, 2007.**

the past decade. In August 2005, he fought for the renewal of the Voting Rights Act. In an impassioned speech at New York's Apollo Theatre, Wonder recalled his own experiences with racism in the 1960s, and recounted a story about his longtime friend Ray Charles, who had only recently passed away. "I remember with one of his early hits, 'I Can't Stop Loving You,' they wouldn't have a picture of him on the cover," he said, as quoted by the *Daily Telegraph*.

> It was a big hit because everybody thought he was white. He didn't outlive racism and hatred. Unfortunately, we will probably not outlive it, either. . . . I'm not OK with having to still march and organize groups of people so that this Voting Act will be signed, and every single American Citizen will have the right to vote without question, for ever.

In 2006, an extension of the Voting Act was signed, ensuring its legal status for another 25 years.

## STILL A FORCE IN MUSIC

In 2007, Wonder launched his first concert tour in 10 years. Dubbed "A Wonder Summer's Night," the tour was a chance for the celebrated musician to continue spreading his message of goodwill in times of trouble. "We have a need for healing in this country," Wonder said in a press conference for the tour. "What better way do we have to thank God than to share in song?" Wonder's shows from London's 02 Arena were captured in the live DVD *Live at Last*, which arrived in stores on March 10, 2009.

Throughout much of 2008, Wonder was a tireless campaigner for Barack Obama during the Illinois senator's bid for the presidency of the United States. In August 2008, during the Democratic National Convention, Wonder performed at Invesco Field in Denver, Colorado, the site of the convention.

His set included a previously unreleased song, "Fear Can't Put Dreams to Sleep," as well as "Signed, Sealed, Delivered (I'm Yours)," a track that had become a sort of theme song for the Obama campaign.

During that time, he also began working on two albums simultaneously. The first, provisionally titled *The Gospel Inspired by Lula*, is a tribute to his late mother. "My whole thing of the title is just saying 'Spreading the good word, the message,'" he explained in an interview with *Billboard*. "I've written a few things on the road and . . . I've had songs throughout the years that I never recorded and so a combination of those songs and some traditional things will make up for the project. And I'm excited about it." The second is tentatively called *Through the Eyes of Wonder* and will be an album recorded from live performances that attempts to show the world what life is like living as a blind man. "What I want to do with our live performances is to create visuals that [give] my take on how I see the world and how most various things affected me," he said.

On July 7, 2009, Wonder performed at the memorial service for Michael Jackson, the legendary pop singer (and fellow Motown artist) who died on June 25, 2009, at the age of 50. Before singing, Wonder addressed the crowd:

## IN HIS OWN WORDS...

**When once asked how he wanted to be remembered, Stevie Wonder responded:**

Either you live to die or you die living. I will die living. I want my legacy to be that everyone I have loved—children, wife, family, fans—knows that I was a lover of life, that I was so very honored to be on this planet, and thankful to be chosen as one of the people that God chose to express not only my feelings, but hopefully the feelings of many people who never had the chance to do so.

This is a moment that I wished to never see come. But as much as I can say that, and mean it, I do know that God is good, and I do know that as much as we feel—and we do— that we need Michael here with us, God must have needed him far more. Michael, I love you and I told you that many times, so I'm at peace with that.

From there, he segued into two songs from his earlier period, "Never Dreamed You'd Leave in Summer" from *Where I'm Coming From* and "They Won't Go When I Go," from *Fulfillingness' First Finale.* At the end of "Never Dreamed You'd Leave in Summer," Wonder altered the lyrics to say, "Michael, why didn't you stay?"

## THE MAN TODAY

Stevie Wonder's career covers five decades, 10 U.S. presidents, and countless scientific and technological advances. The modern world is a far different one than the one that first welcomed the 12-year-old genius to the Motown stage in the early 1960s. But one thing remains the same: Stevie Wonder continues to write, record, produce, and perform, and his musical influence remains undiminished. In fact, in 2006, the hit reality series *American Idol* featured "Stevie Wonder Night," in which all of the 12 contestants were required to sing a song from Wonder's repertoire. The artist himself appeared on the program, performing "My Love Is on Fire" from *A Time to Love.*

Although Stevie Wonder has been a constant presence in music, pop culture, and politics, he feels he still has a lot left to accomplish. Why does he do it? Not for fame, wealth, or accolades. He has had enough of all three to last several lifetimes. Wonder continues to create music for one simple reason: It is what he feels he was created to do. "God heals me through music, the songs that I write," he said. "And I share them because he's given them for everybody."

**1963** *Recorded Live: The 12 Year Old Genius; With a Song in My Heart*

**1964** *Stevie at the Beach*

**1965** *Up-Tight (Everything's Alright)*

**1966** *Down to Earth*

**1967** *I Was Made to Love Her*

**1968** *Eivets Rednow; For Once in My Life*

**1969** *My Cherie Amour*

**1970** *Signed, Sealed and Delivered; Stevie Wonder Live*

**1971** *Where I'm Coming From*

**1972** *Music of My Mind; Talking Book*

**1973** *Innervisions*

**1974** *Fulfillingness' First Finale*

**1976** *Songs in the Key of Life*

**1979** *Journey Through the Secret Life of Plants*

**1980** *Hotter than July*

**1982** *Stevie Wonder's Original Musiquarium*

**1984** *The Woman in Red*

**1985** *In Square Circle*

**1987** *Characters*

**1995** *Conversation Peace*

**1996** *Natural Wonder*

**1997** *Song Review: A Greatest Hits Collection*

**2000** *At the Close of a Century*

**2002** *The Definitive Collection*

**2004** *Best of Stevie Wonder: 20th Century Masters Christmas Collection*

**2005** *A Time to Love*

**2007** *Number 1's*

**1950** Stevie Wonder is born Steveland Hardaway Judkins in Saginaw, Michigan. His mother later changes his name to Steveland Morris.

**1960** Having begun writing songs at eight years old, Wonder is brought to meet Berry Gordy, president of Motown Records, who signs the 10-year-old prodigy to a deal on the spot.

**1962** "I Call It Pretty Music," Wonder's first single, is released.

**1963** "Fingertips—Part 2," a live recording made at Chicago's Regal Theater, is released and goes on to sell more than a million copies.

**1966** *Up-Tight (Everything's Alright)* is released.

**1968** Wonder secretly releases a jazz album under the name Eivets Rednow.

**1969** Wonder meets with President Richard Nixon, who presents the singer with the President's Committee on Employment of Handicapped People's Distinguished Service Award.

**1970** For his work in championing causes for the blind, Wonder is given the Show Business Inspiration Award by Fight for Sight, an organization that promotes research into various diseases of the eye.

**1971** Wonder turns 21 and receives all of his childhood earnings.

**1972** Wonder joins The Rolling Stones on tour.

**1973** While traveling to a show in North Carolina, Wonder is severely injured in a car crash, rendering him comatose for eight days.

**1974** Wonder plays his first solo concert since the accident.

**1975** On March 1, Wonder wins four Grammys, including Album of the Year. On April 5, Wonder's partner, Yolanda Simmons, gives birth to their daughter, Aisha Zakia.

**1976** Wonder signs a $13 million contract renewal with Motown.

**1977** Wonder wins four Grammys, including Album of the Year for *Songs in the Key of Life*.

**1979** Wonder's daughter, Kita Swan Di, is born.

**1980** Wonder performs a U.K. tour, including a six-night sold-out stand at Wembley Arena.

**1982** Wonder records "Ebony and Ivory" with Paul McCartney.

**1984** The city of Detroit awards Wonder the Key to the City; *The Woman in Red* soundtrack is released, featuring his single "I Just Called to Say I Love You."

**1985** Wonder wins the Oscar for "I Just Called to Say I Love You." Wonder teams with Dionne Warwick and Elton John to record "That's What Friends Are For."

**1989** At 38 years old, Stevie Wonder is inducted into the Rock and Roll Hall of Fame.

**1992** Wonder performs on one of Johnny Carson's final episodes of *The Tonight Show*, singing "I'll Be Seeing You."

**1996** Wonder receives an honorary doctorate from the University of Alabama at Birmingham, which unveils its new Stevie Wonder Center for Computing in the Arts; he performs "Seasons of Love" with the cast of the Broadway musical *Rent* for the show's soundtrack album.

**1997** Wonder sits in with producer/singer Babyface on a special edition of *MTV Unplugged*.

**1998** Wonder performs at the White House for President Bill Clinton and Prime Minister Tony Blair of Great Britain.

**2000** The soundtrack to Spike Lee's film *Bamboozled* features two Wonder compositions, "Misrepresented People" and "Some Years Ago."

**2001** Wonder performs at the three hundredth anniversary celebration for the city of Detroit.

**2002**  The opening ceremonies of the Winter Paralympics in Salt Lake City, Utah, feature Wonder as a performer.

**2004**  Wonder receives a Lifetime Achievement Award from *Billboard*.

**2005**  *A Time to Love* is released.

**2006**  Wonder's mother, Lula Mae Hardaway, dies.

**2008**  Wonder receives the NAACP Hall of Fame Award.

**2009**  President Barack Obama presents Wonder with the Library of Congress's Gershwin Prize at a special gala reception at the White House.

Gordy, Berry. *To Be Loved: The Music, the Magic, the Memories of Motown.* New York: Warner Books, 1994.

Haskins, James. *The Story of Stevie Wonder.* New York: Dell Publishing Co., 1976.

Hull, Ted. *The Wonder Years: My Life & Times With Stevie Wonder.* Bangor, Me.: Booklocker.com, 2002.

Love, Dennis, and Stacy Brown. *Blind Faith: The Miraculous Journey of Lula Hardaway, Stevie Wonder's Mother.* New York: Simon & Schuster, 2002.

Werner, Craig. *Higher Ground: Stevie Wonder, Aretha Franklin, Curtis Mayfield and the Rise and Fall of American Soul.* New York: Crown Publishing, 2004.

Williams, Tenley. *Stevie Wonder: Overcoming Adversity.* New York: Chelsea House, 2002.

## WEB SITES

**All Music Guide, Stevie Wonder**
http://www.allmusic.com/eg/amg.dll

**Stevie Wonder Official Site**
http://www.steviewonder.net

**Jeremy K. Brown** has written for numerous magazines and publications, including *Star, Country Music Today, Wizard, Current Biography*, and *WWE Magazine*. He is the editor of the reference book *Warfare in the 21st Century* and has published numerous short stories. He lives in New York with his wife and family.